Arizona's

BEST WILDFLOWER HIKES

The High Country

TEXT AND PHOTOGRAPHY BY
Christine Maxa

WESTCLIFFE PUBLISHERS

www.westcliffepublishers.com

ISBN: 1-56579-428-1

TEXT AND PHOTOGRAPHY: Christine Maxa, © 2002. All rights reserved.
MAP COPYRIGHT: Rebecca Finkel, © 2002. All rights reserved.

EDITOR: Jennie Shortridge
DESIGNER: Rebecca Finkel, F + P Graphic Design, Inc.; Fort Collins, CO
PRODUCTION MANAGER: Craig Keyzer

PUBLISHER: Westcliffe Publishers, Inc.
P.O. Box 1261
Englewood, Colorado 80150
WWW.WESTCLIFFEPUBLISHERS.COM

PRINTED IN: Hong Kong by H & Y Printing, Ltd.

*For more information about other fine books and calendars from
Westcliffe Publishers, please contact your local bookstore, call us
at 1-800-523-3692, write for our free color catalog, or visit us on
the Web at: **www.westcliffepublishers.com**.*

LIBRARY OF CONGRESS CATALOGING-IN-PUBLICATION DATA:

Maxa, Christine.
Arizona's best wildflower hikes / text and photography by Christine Maxa.
p. cm.
Includes bibliographical references and index (v. 1, p.)
Contents: v. 1. The desert.
ISBN 1-56579-427-3
1. Hiking--Arizona--Guidebooks. 2. Wild flowers--Arizona--Guidebooks. 3.
Arizona--Guidebooks. I. Title

GV199.42.A7 M385 2002
917.9104'54--dc21

2001043519

ON THE COVER:
*The Abineau Trail.
Photo by Jerry Sieve.*

PREVIOUS PAGE:
*Scenic views abound on
the Bismarck Lake Trail.*

OPPOSITE:
*The Widforss Trail takes
you to gorgeous views of
the Grand Canyon.*

PLEASE NOTE:
Risk is always a factor in backcountry and high-mountain travel. Many
of the activities described in this book can be dangerous, especially when
weather is adverse or unpredictable and when unforeseen events or
conditions create a hazardous situation. The author has done her best to
provide the reader with accurate information about backcountry travel, as
well as to point out some of its potential hazards. It is the responsibility of
the users of this guide to learn the necessary skills for safe backcountry
travel and to exercise caution in potentially hazardous areas. The author
and publisher disclaim any liability for injury or other damage caused by
backcountry traveling, mountain biking, or performing any other activity
described in this book.

Acknowledgments

To my contacts at the managing agencies who double-checked my work and went the extra mile in obtaining answers to my questions: *Thank you!*

To the botanists who helped identify flowers: Dixie Damrel, Desert Botanical Gardens; Steve Yoder, the Arboretum at Flagstaff; Mitchell White, Apache-Sitgreaves National Forest; Barbara Phillips, Coconino National Forest; Pete Petrie at the Boyce-Thompson Arboretum: *Thank you!*

To Gregory F. Hansen, National Leave No Trace Program Coordinator, USDA Forest Service, for providing information for the "Leave No Trace" section: *Thank you!*

Canyon Creek grows so thickly with wildflowers that the beaten path often gets swallowed up in color.

For Daniel B.

Arizona's

BEST WILDFLOWER HIKES

The High Country

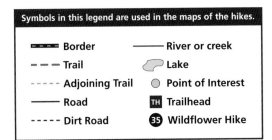

Symbols in this legend are used in the maps of the hikes.	
Border	River or creek
Trail	Lake
Adjoining Trail	Point of Interest
Road	**TH** Trailhead
Dirt Road	**35** Wildflower Hike

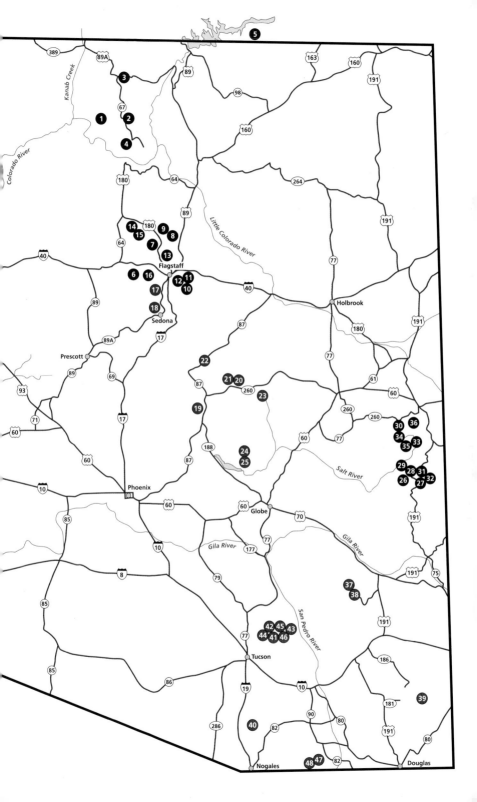

Contents

Wildflower Profiles

Introduction

Arizona's high country has two wildflower seasons. The first comes in the springtime after snowmelt has soaked the mountainslopes. The second, better season starts just after the monsoon rains begin in July.

If the monsoons start late, the wildflowers do, too, and the show of flowers becomes marginal. But if the high country sees a continuous flow of precipitation during the spring and summer, and the temperatures stay above freezing, it's likely to be a banner year. The plants produce big blooms and don't quit until the first frost.

Temperature and precipitation are the keys. Warm temperatures initiate growth, and precipitation amounts determine how much the flowers will grow. Chemicals and nutrients in the soil become accessible to the plants via moisture.

In the high country, trails that follow a perennial stream make the best wildflower hikes. Trails that go through sunny areas with daily rain produce big, too. And trails opened up by fire often produce excellent shows. Most of the trails in this book have these characteristics. There are also several trails that take you into high desert terrain to offer a different variety of wildflowers.

Most of the fieldwork for this book was done during a banner year. If you hike the book's trails on an average or slow year, you may not find the same show of flowers. Also, the same flowers do not always appear in the same places each year. With the variable nature of wildflowers in mind, use this guide as a benchmark for the kind of flowers you may see.

Also keep in mind that this book was written as a hiking guide for hikers who enjoy wildflowers. While wildflower facts were diligently researched and excellent advice and input was received from professional botanists, flower identification can be tricky, even for professionals. Identification keys often vary from expert to expert and there can be tremendous variety within a species. I found Anne Orth Epple's *A Field Guide to the Plants of Arizona* to be the source most conducive to naming the plants. Any incorrect plant identifications are the author's responsibility.

HAPPY HIKING!

*An alpine meadow, surrounded by Arizona's highest peaks,
awaits the hiker at the end of the Abineau Trail.*

How to Use This Guide

With its extraordinarily diverse topography, Arizona has six vegetative life zones: Lower Sonoran, Upper Sonoran, Transition, Canadian, Hudsonian, and Alpine. This book contains hikes located in the Upper Sonoran, Transition, Canadian, and Hudsonian zones. These biomes span from the high desert at 4,500 feet to subalpine meadows at 10,500 feet, and include vegetation such as piñon and ponderosa pines, firs, and spruce.

When planning your wildflower hikes, go beyond considering the spots with the most spectacular photographs or the ones closest to your home. Consider the length and difficulty of the hike (see Appendix B, p. 224, for a list of trails arranged by difficulty). Each hike description includes a Trail Rating from easy to strenuous. These ratings are defined as follows:

- **EASY** trails have well-marked paths and little or no grade, so almost anyone can do these hikes without difficulty.

- **MODERATE** trails are characterized by moderate grades and well-defined paths. Generally, some hiking experience is helpful in navigating these trails.

- **STRENUOUS TRAILS** feature steep grades and generally well-marked paths, but are best suited to experienced hikers in good health.

In addition to the Trail Rating, each hike description includes:

- **TRAIL LENGTH,** which you can often adjust by turning around sooner or walking farther.

- **LOCATION,** such as a town, national park, or refuge.

- **ELEVATION,** including loss or gain.

- **CONTACT** name and phone number so you can check conditions.

- **BLOOM SEASON** and **PEAK BLOOM,** which can vary from year to year.

- **SPECIAL CONSIDERATIONS,** which may include rules, fees, or trail advice (not included for every hike).

- **DIRECTIONS,** from a prominent town, landmark, or highway in the area.

I recommend that you review all these details before setting out on a hiking excursion.

Wildflower names appear in bold type throughout the book for easy identification. Appendix A, p. 220, lists the common and scientific names of the wildflowers mentioned in the text.

Larkspur along the Comfort Spring Trail.

Leave No Trace

BY GREGORY F. HANSEN
National Leave No Trace Program Coordinator, USDA Forest Service

The U.S. Forest Service introduced the idea of Leave No Trace in the 1970s, when the popularity of hiking and backpacking led millions of people out to enjoy their national forests and other public lands. This increased use brought about an overwhelming increase in human impact. Something had to be done to save these special places from literally being "loved to death." The Leave No Trace Program grew out of a need to teach the American people about minimum impact camping and to share with them an attitude of treading lightly on the land. The Leave No Trace concept is much more than just minimum impact camping—it is an awareness, an understanding, of our responsibility and connection to our natural environment.

The following seven principles will help you enjoy your outdoor experience in a way that leaves our public lands unimpaired for future generations. Visits to different environments—desert, mountain, seashore, wetland—each require different Leave No Trace methods. Make the effort to contact a local managing agency before each trip for information about the proper land ethics for that specific area. We can all help protect the natural integrity and value of our precious natural resources by working hard to Leave No Trace.

Leave No Trace Principles

PLAN AHEAD AND PREPARE. Proper trip planning and preparation—including obtaining information about geography and weather—help hikers accomplish trip goals safely and enjoyably while minimizing damage to natural and cultural resources.

TRAVEL AND CAMP ON DURABLE SURFACES. Damage to land occurs when visitors trample vegetation or communities of organisms beyond recovery. The resulting barren areas develop into undesirable soil erosion, trails, and campsites. When hiking, stay on the trail. If you must hike off-trail, hike on the most durable surface (and if you're in a group, spread out).

DISPOSE OF WASTE PROPERLY (PACK IT IN, PACK IT OUT). Whatever you take into the backcountry, take out. Double-check your rest and lunch spots for anything left behind. To help prevent disease and contamination of water sources, dispose of human waste at least 200 feet from water, trails, and campsites (use a cat hole dug 6 to 8 inches deep).

Wildflowers greet you at the beginning of the Horton Creek Trail.

LEAVE WHAT YOU FIND. Leave rocks, plants, animals, archaeological artifacts, and other objects as you find them. Examine—but do not touch—cultural or historical structures. This preserves the past and allows other hikers a sense of discovery.

MINIMIZE CAMPFIRE IMPACTS. If you must build a fire, the most important consideration is the potential for resource damage. Make a small fire using dead or downed wood. Whenever possible, use an existing campfire ring in a well-placed campsite. Skip the fire in areas where wood is scarce, such as in higher elevations, in heavily used areas with limited wood supply, or in desert settings. Call the managing agency listed under Contact to inquire about fire restrictions; in some areas, campfires are prohibited.

RESPECT WILDLIFE. Quick movements and loud noises are stressful to animals. To avoid disturbing them, try to observe animals from afar. If your presence alters their normal activity, you are too close. Give animals a wide berth, especially during breeding, nesting, and birthing seasons.

BE CONSIDERATE OF OTHER VISITORS. While hiking, keep in mind:
- Travel in small groups.
- Keep noise levels down. Let nature's sounds prevail.
- Wear clothing with colors that blend with the environment.
- Respect private property; leave gates the way you found them (opened or closed).

A wild geranium is sheltered by a fallen log on the Vault Mine Trail.

On the Trail

TIPS FOR VIEWING WILDFLOWERS

- Call the contact numbers provided to inquire about wildflower displays.
- Bring plenty of water and food.
- Carry a magnifying glass to help you see fine details of the flowers.
- Don't pick flowers, buds, or seed plants. Some are on endangered lists and are illegal to pick.
- Don't stop on the freeway or park on the side of roads to take pictures.
- Watch for the wildflower pollinators: bees, butterflies, hummingbirds, ants, bats, and beetles (but keep out of their way).
- Be aware that some wildflowers cause allergic reactions.

RULES AND REGULATIONS ABOUT NATIVE PLANTS

According to Ellen Bilbrey, public information officer with Arizona State Parks, native plant laws protect a variety of plants throughout Arizona and require that people not harm these plants. This includes digging them up, shooting them, stealing plant skeletons, collecting seeds, or picking flowers.

About 30 different plants and almost all cacti are on the native plant protected list. There are civil penalties and fines ranging up to $2,500 and six months in jail for violating these laws.

For plants inside state and national parks, the laws are even more stringent. You can't collect plants, harm plants or animals, pick up any type of plant skeleton, collect wood, pick up archaeological or historical objects, or even take rocks from the parks.

SAFETY AROUND SNAKES

Encounters with snakes occur less frequently in the high country compared to the desert, but they do exist in mountains and forests. Rory Aiken, public information officer with the Arizona Game & Fish Department, gives these tips:

- Stay on established trails. Snakes are less likely to hang around on worn human trails, and you can clearly see the ground in front of you.
- Use a walking stick. It gives you better balance, makes additional noise to warn the snake of your approach, and extends out in front of your body.
- Keep children and dogs close by and preferably behind you.
- Put your hands and feet only where you can see them.
- Don't pick up or try to move any snake you encounter, not even by throwing objects at it. Instead, walk slowly around the snake. A good rule of thumb is to keep at least six feet away.

WHAT TO DO IF A BEAR CROSSES YOUR PATH

High-country trails bring you to black bear country and sighting one can be an exciting experience. Most wild bears will detect and avoid humans, but

when a bear has become accustomed to humans and their food, it may not run away. The exciting moment can turn to conflict. Most conflicts between humans and black bears happen because of human-supplied foods. When you're in the high country, make sure all of your food and toiletries are inaccessible to bears. Here's what to do if a conflict arises:

- Do not run. Slowly back away facing the bear.
- Don't approach the bear.
- Don't get between a mother and her cubs.
- Keep children and pets close to your side.
- Make noise—clap hands, yell, whistle, or break sticks.
- Fight back if a bear attacks you.
- Stand upright, waving your arms. Don't crouch or kneel.

MONSOON SEASON

During summer, usually from July to mid-September, Arizona experiences its monsoon season. Thunderstorms occur when warm, moist air from the Gulf of Mexico travels into the state. In the high country, these storms often occur daily. A hike started in morning sunshine may see clouds gathering by midmorning, a thunderstorm around noon, and calm skies by sunset. People living in Arizona's mountain towns talk about being able to set their clocks by daily rainstorms.

During these storms, temperatures can drop 20–30 degrees, hail may form, and flash floods may thunder down creeks and drainage areas. Lightning strikes, hypothermia, and drowning are all potential dangers. The best way to avoid storms during monsoon season is to start your hike at first light and plan to end it by noon.

HOW TO AVOID LIGHTNING STRIKES

An average of four people die of lightning strikes per year in Arizona during the short monsoon season. The Mogollon Rim has the second highest occurrence of lightning in the United States. You can decrease your chances of becoming a prime target for lightning if you:

- Stay out from under trees.
- Head for the lowest spot, crouch down, and curl into a ball.
- Don't lie on the ground—lightning travels into the ground and you want as little contact as possible with its 50,000-degree bolts.

HOW TO AVOID HYPOTHERMIA

Hypothermia becomes a threat during high-country storms. The combination of wet clothes and dramatic drops in temperature makes hypothermia—core body temperature below safe levels—a real danger. Hypothermia takes place most often in temperatures between 30 and 50 degrees and is the number one killer of outdoor recreation enthusiasts. To avoid hypothermia:

- Stay dry. Always take rain gear on every hike, and wear it. Wet clothes lose 90 percent of their insulation value.
- Bring a synthetic jacket or wool sweater to keep you warm when the temperature drops.
- Bring waterproof matches or a lighter in case you need a fire for warmth.
- Eat high-carbohydrate snacks to help fuel your body.

HOW TO AVOID FLASH FLOODS

Water levels rise quickly in high-country creeks during thunderstorms. An easy rock-hop across a creek at the start of your hike can turn into a major production during or after a rainstorm. Footing may become slippery on stepping-stones, and high-level waters may turn murky and swallow them entirely. Currents become too strong to wade through—water 3 feet deep traveling 3 feet per second can knock an average-sized man down. If you find yourself stuck during high water:

- Use a walking stick to help keep your balance when crossing high, fast-moving creeks.
- Make sure your footing is secure before taking the next step.
- Try to cross near objects you can hold on to, such as tree branches or boulders.
- Never cross water with depths more than 3 feet traveling 3 feet or more per second.

*Wildflower
Hike 1*

Parissawampitts Point: Rainbow Rim Trail

This trail shows color from many wildflower species and offers great views of the Grand Canyon.

This westernmost section of the 18-mile-long Rainbow Rim Trail gets a striking start. The trail descends a hillside filled with wildflower color that leads to the edge of the Grand Canyon and its panorama of stratified knolls, terraces, and points in the gorge. The hike then heads east to Parissawampitts Canyon along the rim and through ponderosa pine parks separated by flower-filled meadows. The trail ends at Fence Point with more fabulous views of the Grand Canyon.

The golden sheen on the hike's opening meadow comes from **snakeweed. Indian paintbrush, golden-beard penstemon,** and **skyrocket** interrupt the glow with red blossoms. The easy-to-spot purple flower heads of **Wheeler thistle** stand above the crowd of flowers on the hillside. Look for more purple flowers on **two-tone owl's clover** and **narrow-leaf penstemon.**

Trail Rating	Moderate
Trail Length	3–5.5 miles one way
Location	North Rim of the Grand Canyon
Elevation	7,550–7,700 feet
Contact	Kaibab National Forest, North Kaibab Ranger District, 928-643-7395
Bloom Season	June–September
Peak Bloom	August
Directions	From Jacob Lake, drive south on AZ 67 26.5 miles and turn right (west) on FR 22 at DeMotte Park. In a mile you'll reach an intersection. Go straight ahead and the road becomes West Side Road (FR 22). Continue northwest about 9 miles to FR 206; turn left (south) on FR 206 and go 3.5 miles to FR 214. Turn right (west) and drive 8 miles to the trailhead.

The trail reaches the rim of the Grand Canyon, turns left, and follows the edge of the canyon. At about mile 0.1, the path scrapes through a prickly corridor of **Wheeler thistle** and **skyrocket** to a shallow ravine filled with Gambel oaks. In the shadows, **yarrow, Richardson's geranium,** and **sego lily** grow gangly stems reaching for sun dapples. **Meadow rue** dangles tasseled blossoms. Watch for **sego lily** until the trail exits the oak grove and moves back into the sun.

The path makes an S-curve leading to a window in the pine trees that opens to a view of the Grand Canyon. **Cliff rose** bushes may still have their pale-yellow blooms, but early bloomers may display their feathered fruit by August. **Golden-beard penstemon** makes a striking contrast against wan green **sagebrush** bushes wafting their medicinal pungence. Farther down the path, **yellow-flowered buckwheat** mixes with **common snakeweed.** You can tell the two apart by the hues of their blossoms. **Yellow-flowered buckwheat** has fluorescent yellow flowers, while **snakeweed** has golden blossoms.

The trailsides stay colorful with **golden-beard penstemon, Wheeler thistle, yellow-flowered buckwheat,** and **white top clover. Cliff rose** crowds around the path, still edging the canyon rim. A colony of **Indian paintbrush** mingles their coral blooms in **sagebrush** as the trail curves to follow the contour of the canyon rim.

The trailsides turn grassy as the trail pulls away from the rim at about mile 0.4. **White top clover** follows first, then **Wright's deervetch, red-root**

buckwheat, and **cinquefoil** joins. As the trail coasts down a hillside to a meadow, **western blue flax** and **silver-stem lupine** appear in a clearing on the left. If you look south, you can see the stratified cliffs of the Grand Canyon through the ponderosa pine trees.

The meadow turns grassy at about mile 0.5, crowding out most of the wildflowers except for **red-root buckwheat** and **common snakeweed.** Then the shade from ponderosa pines thins the grass as the trees grow more thickly around the trail with **silver-stem lupine.** A gathering of Gambel oak trees draws **sego lily** back to the trail.

Back in full sun, the landscape turns grassy again with **Wheeler thistle, Wright's deervetch,** and **red-root buckwheat** gathering around the trail. **Golden aster** makes an appearance here, too. Its quarter-sized gold daisy blossoms top hairy stems of wavy leaves. Just before the trail wends through another Gambel oak grove, daisy-shaped **goldeneye** and the pea flowers of **birdsfoot lotus** display yellow-colored blossoms.

In the shadows of a shallow ravine, **verileaf phacelia** edges the trail just ahead of strapping aspen trees. The trademark phacelia curl of blossoms tops hairy stems and leaves. A colony of **mullein** crowds around the path; their elongated clusters of yellow flowers look pretty on columns of velvet leaves. **Wild geranium** lays shocks of purple at their feet.

The trail breaks from the shady cover of trees just before it drops into Parissawampitts Canyon. Little **Hill's lupine** edges the trail, and **narrow-leaf penstemon** forms clusters that continue to the canyon floor. On the downhill

SEGO LILY
Calochortus nuttallii

Calochortus, the sego lily's scientific name, means "beautiful grass"—a fitting name when you study the exquisite white or lavender-colored flower that tops a slender stem surrounded by a few grassy leaves. The flower has three satiny petals painted with purple banding at their bases.

Indians ate the sego lily's nutritious bulbs, and taught the Mormons who first arrived in Utah to include them in their diets. Starchy, with a consistency like potatoes, the bulbs are a favorite food of bears out of hibernation. They leave telltale pockmarks in the ground where they've dug them up.

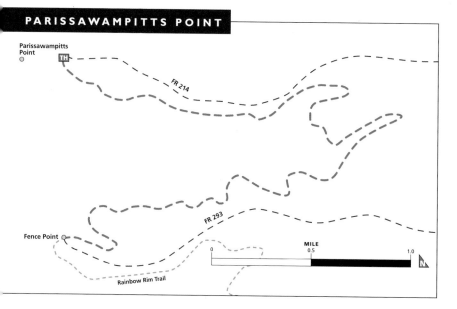

into the canyon, **western blue flax** meets with **wild geranium**, and **Wheeler thistle** continues its ubiquitous show.

About midway on the downhill, a corridor of **mullein** purpled with **Wheeler thistle** and **wild geranium** forms around the trail. You may notice **antelope horns** and **common mallow** beneath **mullein** stalks. Look, too, for the light-orange tube flowers of **grand collomia.**

Continuing downhill, the trail passes sunny slopes full of **golden-beard penstemon, skyrocket,** and **Cooper's goldflower.** The canyon, narrow and moist from Parissawampitts Spring, provides an environment that coaxes aspen trees and forest-loving wildflowers to proliferate. At the canyon floor, full of **wandbloom penstemon** and **Cooper's goldflower,** the trail almost immediately begins its climb back out.

Plains beebalm edges the trail at the onset of the climb. If you snap one of the toothed leaves from this typical square-stemmed mint family member, you may detect a peppery mint smell. As the trail climbs, you quickly notice the **Arizona rose, yarrow, Richardson's geranium,** and **osha** that congregate along this moist, shady stretch. Watch for **sego lily** and **Rocky Mountain columbine,** too. **Indian paintbrush** flames in sunny spots.

When the trail tops out at about mile 3, it leaves a number of the wildflowers behind as it threads through a ponderosa forest interspersed with Gambel oak groves. The rim makes a good turnaround point for a wildflower hike. However, you may continue on the trail 2.5 more miles to Fence Point.

Crystal Spring: Arizona Trail

Meadows and forests are side by side on this colorful hike.

This section of the near-complete Arizona Trail, which when finished will stretch about 800 miles from the northern edge of Arizona to the state's southernmost tip, was the first nonexisting portion of the trail constructed. The trail travels through forests of mixed conifers and aspen trees separated by alpine meadows. These meadows fill with wildflowers, especially after the summer rains kick in.

The route starts on a paved walkway in a sun-drenched meadow that brings you, after 0.1 mile, to the edge of North Canyon at the East Rim

Trail Rating	Moderate
Trail Length	2.5 miles one way
Location	North Rim of the Grand Canyon
Elevation	8,200–8,800 feet
Contact	Kaibab National Forest, North Kaibab Ranger District, 928-643-7395
Bloom Season	July–September
Peak Bloom	August
Directions	From Jacob Lake, drive 24.8 miles south on AZ 67 to FR 610. Turn left (east) and drive about 1 mile. The road will bend northeast onto FR 611. Stay on FR 611 and drive about 3 miles to the trailhead.

Overlook. At the rim, Marble Canyon shows up like a gash in the Colorado Plateau. Domelike Navajo Mountain rises in the east and Kaiparowits Plateau runs along the northern horizon.

The meadow's blend of wildflowers matches the striking panoramic scene. **Cooper's goldflower** and **cinquefoil** glow gold. **Red-root buckwheat** waves pink-toned floral clusters on spindly stems. **Indian paintbrush** flames red. **Skyrocket,** usually orange-red, paints deep-pink patterns across the meadow. Purple daisy-like **aspen fleabane** dots the field and follows the trail to Crystal Spring.

At a T-intersection, mile 0.1, turn right onto the Arizona Trail. The trail, now unpaved, continues in the meadow paralleling North Canyon. **Fendler's sandwort** sprinkles across the east trailside, and **skyrocket** and **cinquefoil** the west trailside. The path narrows to a single track and ducks in and out of stands of mixed conifers separated by meadows.

The sunny pockets in the stands of trees encourage **aspen fleabane, goldeneye,** and **Richardson's geranium** to gather in them. The meadows draw the variety of flowers the hike started with.

By mile 0.5, the trail enters an aspen-fir forest. The moist and shady environment harbors a different variety of wildflowers. **Meadow rue** and **verileaf phacelia** feel at home in the forest. In sunny dapples, look for **Richardson's geranium, yarrow, aspen fleabane, Indian paintbrush,** and **golden-beard penstemon. Osha** shows white flowered umbels, which progress to fruit that looks like dill seeds.

The mix of dark green conifers and aspen trees' argentine trunks creates a particularly refreshing realm. The colorful red walls of North Canyon show through occasional breaks in the trees.

At about mile 1.2, the trail descends toward the head of North Canyon. You may see **woodland pinedrops** along the downhill. The forest thins as the trail nears North Canyon, coaxing **Indian paintbrush, many-flowered gromwell,** and **Richardson's geranium** to appear in the sunny spots. A line of **golden-beard penstemon** edges the trail as it bends into a sun-drenched slope full of **bristly hiddenflower.**

RED-ROOT BUCKWHEAT

Eriogonum racemosum

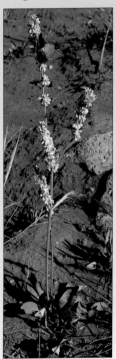

Arizona has more than 50 species of *eriogonum*, members of the buckwheat family. The plants have a propensity to adapt to different soil conditions so succinctly, they often develop into a different species.

The scientific name of *eriogonum* comes from a Greek derivative. The meaning, "woolly knees," refers to the woolly joints on many species' stems. Red-root buckwheat displays a cluster of white or pinkish flowers atop a spindly stem. Its basal leaves have a felt surface. You can often find red-root buckwheat spreading across clearings in high-country pine forests.

Star Solomon's seal surrounds the wooden post marking the trail's junction with the North Canyon Trail. You may spot several different **penstemons** at the junction, such as **wandbloom, Whipple's,** and **golden-beard.**

The path drops into a long meadow at mile 1.5 that fills immediately with wildflowers. This meadow, like most of the surrounding ones in the area, was formed from a small valley. At night, the cooler air settles in the valley and is too cold for trees to survive. Consequently, the treeline edges the depression where the air temperature is more conducive to tree growth.

At the beginning of the meadow, **wandbloom penstemon** mixes in with a sprawling colony of **silver-stem lupine.** As the trail travels through the grassy vale, **Cooper's goldflower** sends up golden clusters on lance-leaved stalks. **Sandwort** and **yarrow** dot the

CRYSTAL SPRING

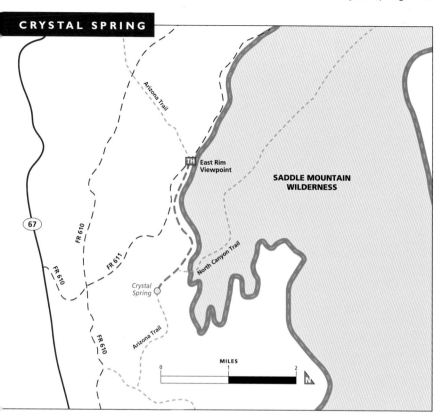

blue spread of **silver-stem lupine** white, and **Indian paintbrush** add splotches of red. **Mountain parsley** and **wandbloom penstemon** often appear near fir trees along the path.

A log fence surrounds still-active Crystal Spring. If you drink the water, be sure to filter it first. You may continue another 4.5 miles on this section of the Arizona Trail to the boundary of Grand Canyon National Park, or return the way you came.

Big Ridge Tank: Arizona Trail

Wildflowers brighten the meadows of the Big Ridge Tank section of the Arizona Trail.

This brief section of the 800-mile-long Arizona Trail travels through ponderosa parks to Big Ridge Tank. The tank gets its name from a rise in the plateau just east of the trail called Big Ridge.

The route starts on an easy climb up a sun-drenched hillside. Before you start, take a look around the parking area for **evening primrose** and **New Mexico vervain** edging the roadside. **Cinquefoil** mixes with **red-root buckwheat** and **narrow-leaf penstemon** at the very start of the trail, then follows the path as it starts its journey to Big Ridge Tank.

Trail Rating	Easy
Trail Length	1.5 miles
Location	Jacob Lake
Elevation	7,920–8,050 feet
Contact	Kaibab National Forest, North Kaibab Ranger District, 928-643-7395
Bloom Season	July–September
Peak Bloom	August
Directions	From Jacob Lake, drive east on US 89A approximately 3 miles to the signed trailhead on the south side of the highway.

Climbing the hill, the trail cuts through a cover of golden clusters of **common snakeweed**. Yellow-flowered **Wright's deervetch** appears throughout the trail, and sticks close to the path during the hillside climb. Splashes of red from **golden-beard penstemon, skyrocket**, and **Indian paintbrush** complement the golden glow.

The white star flowers with pink anthers that look, at a quick glance, like pink spots on each of the five petals, are **Fendler's sandwort**. Before the trail reaches the hilltop at mile 0.2, you may identify over a dozen different wildflowers.

As the trail tops out, **silver-stem lupine** display fragrant pea blossoms. Smaller **Hill's lupine** appears when the path levels out. **Cooper's goldflower** and **Wright's deervetch** cover the forest floor. Watch for a **mullein** colony surrounding a dozen tree stumps. The colony shows several stages of the columnar plant, from velvet-leaved sprouts to mature plants topped with yellow flower spikes to browned skeletons.

In another 100 feet, a large colony of **silver-stem lupine** fills a sunny clearing. **Fendler's sandwort** returns to the trail in waves. You might miss the **many-flowered gromwell** in the spread of **Wright's deervetch** unless you watch for their attractive yellow flower clusters.

By mile 0.4, the trail coasts downhill. A douse of sunshine on the hillside coaxes a colorful spread of **common snakeweed** and **Indian paintbrush**. Just before the trail joins a dirt road at mile 0.5, **many-flowered gromwell, meadow rue**, and **narrow-leaf penstemon** gather around the rocky drop into the road. Turn left onto the road to continue.

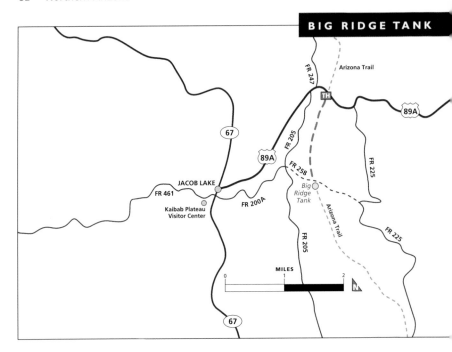

BIG RIDGE TANK

Arizona Trail

FR 247

TH

89A

67

FR 205

89A

FR 258

FR 225

JACOB LAKE

FR 461

Big Ridge Tank

Kaibab Plateau Visitor Center

FR 200A

Arizona Trail

FR 205

FR 225

MILES

0   1   2

67

Bristly hiddenflower and **many-flowered gromwell** surround the road. Both of these wildflowers belong to the borage family, and both have bristly hairs on their leaves. **Bristly Hiddenflower** has curls of white flowers and a more noticeable cover of hairs. **Many-flowered gromwell** has funnel-shaped flowers. **Red-root buckwheat** comes back with more **silver-stem lupine.**

The road bends east momentarily, then resumes south again to a gradual climb up a mild slope. **Silver-stem lupine** multiplies so thickly you can smell its sweetness in the air.

The *lupinus* genus got its name from *lupus*, the Latin word for wolf, referring to the belief that lupine ravages the land like wolves. On the contrary, *lupinus* adds nitrogen into the soil, which fortifies plants. The *lupinus* also got the name *Pisum lupinum*, referring to their bitter peas that were supposedly fit only for wolves. The peas become palatable only after several boilings.

This process provoked the Greek philosopher Zeno to compare himself to lupine seeds—when he was well soaked (with wine), he was less bitter. Zeno practiced Stoicism, a theology that teaches the universe has a soul and whose followers accept the destiny it dictates for them. Zeno, who liked to eat green figs and lounge in the sun, must have realized that his lot was a life of leisure.

Near a curve in the road, about mile 0.7, **white prairie clover** appears. Its white clusters have prominent gold anthers often topped with a bud spike.

The sun-drenched clearing on the west side of the trail at mile 0.75 attracts **golden-beard penstemon** and **Indian paintbrush** to the prevailing spread of **silver-stem lupine**. Veer right at a fork in the road at mile 0.8.

Wright's deervetch, silver-stem lupine, yarrow, and Fendler's sandwort are the predominant florals here with **silver-stem lupine** persisting until about mile 0.9. The blue haze of lupines is interrupted occasionally by spurts of **common snakeweed** and **Indian paintbrush.**

At mile 1.3, the trail breaks from the shade of the ponderosas. Just before the trail crosses a dirt road, you may see a colony of **many-flowered gromwell.** On the other side of the dirt road, a mix of **silver-stem lupine, golden-beard penstemon, Indian paintbrush,** and **common snakeweed** add a variety of color to the trailsides.

The trail quickly drops in and out of a narrow ravine where **Richardson's geranium** settles. Once in a large sunny meadow on the other side of the ravine, and just before Big Ridge Tank, the trail passes tall **winged buckwheat, red-root buckwheat,** and **silver-stem lupine. Richardson's geranium** gathers under the **currant** bushes next to Big Ridge Tank.

Take a moment to walk along the south side of the tank. **New Mexico vervain** lines the pathway and **prostrate vervain** lies right on the trail. **Arizona rose** bushes tangle in the rugged wooden fence around the tank. You might find pretty, scented, pink rose blossoms if you hike in June or July.

You may continue on the Arizona Trail or return the way you came.

MULLEIN
Verbascum thapsus

The stellate hairs on mullein give this towering plant its alternate names of felt plant and velvet plant. During the biennial's first year, the plant develops a rosette of large, sage-colored leaves. The plant sends up a several-foot-tall flower stalk of five-petaled yellow flowers with orange stamens the subsequent year.

The European import has a prolific nature and appears all over the state, gravitating to disturbed areas or roadsides. The plant has many uses. Colonists and Indians used its leaves, soft to the touch, to line their footwear. Hopi Indians smoked the leaves to rebalance the mind. Herbalists make a tea from the leaves to relieve coughs and hoarseness.

Widforss Trail

Grand Canyon panoramas make up the Widforss Trail's journey.

The Widforss Trail is named for landscape painter Gunnar Widforss, who lived and painted in the Grand Canyon from 1921 to 1934. He had a heart attack near El Tovar and was buried in the Grand Canyon Cemetery.

The Widforss Trail follows along the North Rim of the Grand Canyon inside Grand Canyon National Park. The trail drops several times in and out of forested drainages as it heads to a scenic spot called Widforss Point.

The trail starts in Harvey Meadow, stepping right into a spread of wildflowers that tangle in the meadow's tall grasses, such as **wandbloom penstemon, red-root buckwheat, Cooper's goldflower, buttercup**, and **Wright's deervetch**. Stalks of **bristly hiddenflower** show curls of white flowers.

Trail Rating	Moderate
Trail Length	5 miles one way
Location	North Rim of the Grand Canyon
Elevation	7,900–8,100 feet
Contact	National Park Service, 928-638-7888
Bloom Season	July–September
Peak Bloom	August
Special Considerations	The National Park Service charges a $20 entrance fee good for up to one week from the day of purchase.
Directions	From Jacob Lake, drive south on AZ 67, about 30 miles to the North Rim entrance. Continue 9.7 miles to the signed turnoff for the Widforss Trail; turn right (west), and drive 0.6 mile to the trailhead.

Meadow rue and **false Solomon's seal** stay close to conifers. **Yarrow** and **Fendler's sandwort** sprinkle white blossoms.

The trail leaves most of these flowers behind as it climbs above the meadow into a forest of conifers. In the early part of the morning, you might catch glimpses of wild turkey in the meadow or hear deer crashing through thickets in the forest.

Kaibab limestone outcroppings along the trail have **golden-beard penstemon** growing in dents and air holes on the rock. You may see crinoid fossils in the limestone, as well.

The first panorama of the canyon appears at about mile 0.25. **Wheeler thistle, golden-beard penstemon,** and **Indian paintbrush** hug the rim at the view point. The wildflowers disappear as the trail drops into a ravine. It lands on the moist drainage bottom, about mile 0.6, in a colony of **Richardson's geranium, yarrow,** and **many-flowered gromwell. Bracken fern,** also here, is the most common fern in Arizona.

Back on the rim, the trail reveals an outstanding view of the canyon. **Wheeler thistle** and **golden-beard penstemon** crowd in the clearing. But the trail drops again, in and out of another drainage. It then tops out on the rim, about mile 1.25, and heads into a spread of **silver-stem lupine. Bristly hiddenflower** stand tall in the lupine. **Red elderberry** bushes hang in back of the florals.

As the trail contours the rim, **golden aster** outlines the trailsides with deep gold, then melds heavily with **silver-stem lupine's** indigo. An aspen stand makes a soothing backdrop for these wildflowers. Look for **Fendler's ceanothus**, **cliff rose**, and **green leaf manzanita** hugging the rim.

Once again, the trail leaves the rim to drop into a drainage. The drainage floor, about mile 1.7, harbors a mix of white flowers among the dark green conifers: **verileaf phacelia**, **Richardson's geranium**, **osha**, and **yarrow**. They twist with the trail in the drainage, but stay behind as the trail climbs out into a palette of color on the rim: more ruddy vistas and carpets of **golden aster** and **silver-stem lupine** sprinkled with **golden-beard penstemon**.

Silver-stem lupine follows the trail on its next venture away from the rim, in and out of a small drainage. Back on the rim, watch for **red elderberry** bushes along the trail. **Cliff rose** competes with scrub oak for a spot along the rim.

At mile 2.5, the trail pulls away from the rim to head into another drainage. **Silver-stem lupine** covers the sunny slope into the drainage. Most of the groundcover along the trail as it climbs out of the

YARROW

Achillea millefolium var. *lanulosa*

Europeans brought yarrow to America, and the fern-leaved plant spread easily throughout the land. In Arizona, you find it in high-country fields and roadsides. Cattle resist eating the plant's bitter leaves, which impart a disagreeable taste to their milk. Humans, however, have put the plant to use, utilizing it medicinally and magically.

Europeans used yarrow to allay bleeding, which gave it alternate names of bloodwort and wound-wort. The plant's scientific name, *Achillea*, comes from Achilles. On the advice of mythological healer Chiron, Achilles used yarrow to heal his wounded soldiers. This lore made the plant popular with battlefield surgeons, who incorporated yarrow in their treatment of bullet wounds as late as the Civil War.

Europeans also used yarrow to protect themselves from evil by burning the plant on the eve of St. John's Day. Sometimes they would light windward fires in fields of yarrow so the smoke would infiltrate and protect their town.

Herbalists still use yarrow for bleeding problems. They also combine yarrow flowers with elder flowers to make a tea that promotes a sweat to relieve a cold or flu.

WIDFORSS TRAIL

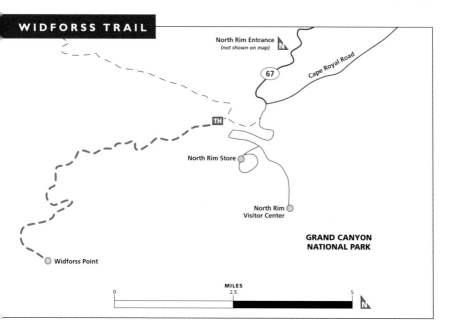

North Rim Entrance
(not shown on map)

67

Cape Royal Road

TH

North Rim Store

North Rim
Visitor Center

**GRAND CANYON
NATIONAL PARK**

Widforss Point

MILES
2.5

0   5

drainage is **creeping barberry**. In the spring, the creeping shrub sprouts clusters of yellow flowers that produce purple berries by summer.

Silver-stem lupine crowds the trail as it arrives back on the rim at about mile 3. A bit farther, you may spot the orange funnel flowers on a colony of **grand collomia**. These attractive flowers have a peculiar feature that inspired their name, which comes from the Greek word *kolla*, meaning glue. The seeds of these flowers have a high mucous content. The mucous diffuses when the seeds are dropped in water and clouds around the seeds.

At mile 3.5, the trail passes a limestone wall that juts from the rim. If you take a moment to study the wall, you may see what looks like an erosion-sculpted table and a window propped on its top. Then the trail drops into a ravine that parallels the rim.

The atmosphere in the ravine turns moody with the argentine glow from a forest of aspens contrasted with a nonstop carpet of **silver-stem lupine**. **Yarrow** and **Richardson's geranium** dot the groundcover with their white blossoms, and **goldeneye** adds gold flecks.

The trail climbs out of the ravine at mile 4, then takes its time heading for the rim. Wildflowers congregate in the sunny clearings of the forested stretch, forming colorful patches of **skyrocket**, **Indian paintbrush**, and **golden aster**. The trail ends at Widforss Point. Return the way you came.

North Rainbow Trail

This trail features beautiful western redbud trees.

The North Rainbow Trail to Rainbow Bridge, just over the state line in Utah, traverses a spectacular red rock landscape nubby with piñon and juniper trees, blue-green leaved blackbrush, and bright green reeds of ephedra. The trail passes swirling sandstone formations and sheer cliffs, winds through several canyons, and covers miles of bench country to the 290-foot-high Rainbow Bridge, the world's largest natural bridge situated in a tiny national monument at the end of the trail. The salmon-colored bridge spans 275 feet across the teal waters that flow into Lake Powell.

Hiking the whole trail requires a backpack, and is considered moderately challenging. But you may do a day hike along the trail as well. A boat ride

Trail Rating	Easy (boat shuttle)—strenuous
Trail Length	Up to 14 miles one way
Location	From Page, across the state line in Utah
Elevation	3,700–5,200 feet
Contact	The Navajo Nation, 928-871-7762
Bloom Season	Mid-March–September
Peak Bloom	Mid-March–mid-April and August
Special Considerations	The Navajo Nation requires a permit fee of $5 per day per hiker to hike the trail. You may purchase the permit through The Navajo Nation, Recreational Resource Department, Box 308, Window Rock, AZ, 86515, or call 928-871-7762.
Directions	To access the trail via boat, one-way tourboat rides to or from Rainbow Bridge are $50 per person, adult or child, and are available May through September. Advance reservations are necessary. Call 928-645-1070.
	From Page, drive southeast on AZ 98 about 52 miles to Navajo 16 and turn left (north). Drive about 33 miles to a fork in the road, and veer right, staying on Navajo 16; continue another 8.1 miles, crossing into Utah, and head north onto a primitive road requiring four-wheel-drive; drive 4.3 miles to the trailhead.

to the bridge, then a few hours' hike into Bridge Canyon gets you to the heart of the canyon country and the best display of wildflowers, especially western redbud trees. The magenta flowers against the red rock walls are exquisite.

Starting from the north trailhead, the trail takes about 1 mile to drop in and out of an unnamed crevice and the two arms of Cha Canyon. **Indian paintbrush** appears early, along with **locoweed** and **stemless evening primrose.** These wildflowers continue throughout the trail.

As the trail drops into the chasms, look for **Utah serviceberry** to line the pathway. The bush belongs to a group of plants in the Navajo culture called medicine twigs or life medicines. Navajos generally pick herbs just before they use them. But not the life medicines. Herbalists always have these herbs on hand—dried, stored, and ready for use when they need them. **Utah serviceberry** is a Navajo remedy for stomach ailments.

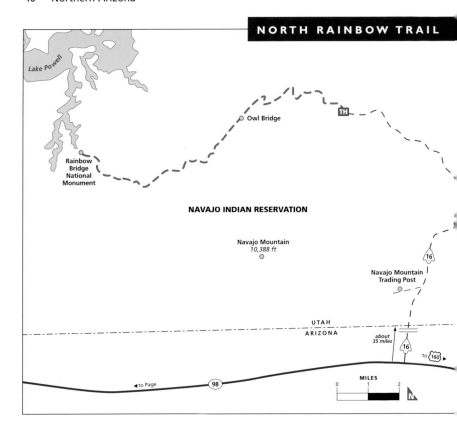

NORTH RAINBOW TRAIL

Lake Powell

Owl Bridge

TH

Rainbow Bridge National Monument

NAVAJO INDIAN RESERVATION

Navajo Mountain
10,388 ft

Navajo Mountain Trading Post

16

UTAH
ARIZONA

about 35 miles

16

to 160 ▶

◀ to Page   98

MILES
0   1   2

N

Utah serviceberry often associates with the fragrant **cliff fendler bush** (also called mock orange) and **cliff rose** bushes. These bushes appear on the way in and out of the canyons.

You may smell **cliff rose** before you see it as you descend into Bald Rock Canyon at mile 3. The trail drops haphazardly on a long, steep descent into the canyon, then levels out once in the canyon.

Year-round water streams down the bedrock canyon floor that wends beneath massive sandstone walls carved with alcoves. **Western wallflower** and **Indian paintbrush** add orange and coral color to the dark red canyon. **Western peppergrass** mounds snow-white clusters along the banks of a creek. Both **western wallflower** and **western peppergrass** belong to the mustard family and share the family's distinct features of four-petaled flowers that produce seedpods.

The route between Bald Rock and Nasja canyons makes an animated journey across slickrock demarcated by cairns, juniper logs, and lines of sandstone rocks. John Wetherill, who explored the area in the early 1920s and led expeditions to Rainbow Bridge, called this area "The Inferno" because of its steepness and the dangerous slickrock mounds, or "baldheads."

Golden-beard penstemon and **western wallflower** cling to sandy patches gathered in depressions in the slickrock. A panorama to the north shows off a dramatic slickrock landscape with the Henry Mountains in the background.

When the trail drops into Surprise Valley at mile 5.5, **sandpuff** lines the path. The round clusters of white flowers top prostrate stems. The Navajos consider the plant a good-luck charm, and some carry it for protection.

Within a short distance, the trail passes a primitive camp next to a perennial stream. The anomalous picnic bench in the camp was brought in decades ago to service tours to the bridge.

Nasja Canyon, located at mile 6, is the largest canyon along the trail and also the most beautiful. **Skyrocket, sandpuff,** and several species of **penstemon** line the trail while towering sandstone walls weep with seeps and showcase arches and alcoves. After a wet winter, Nasja Canyon can have over two dozen different wildflowers.

A watchful hiker will notice Owl Bridge at the eastern end of the canyon. **Western redbud** trees color the trail at the west end of the canyon. If you hike when **western redbud** first starts blooming, you won't see their kidney-shaped leaves. The leaves develop after the blooms appear. The Navajos use the leaves as incense for certain chants.

Patches of yellow **phlox** make for a pretty sight along

WESTERN REDBUD
Cercis occidentalis

If you hike in the canyonways of northern Arizona in early spring, you may see rosy shocks of color against the canyon walls. The color comes from western redbud trees, one of the high desert's prettiest floral sights.

The bright, rose-pink flowers of the western redbud look like their relatives in the pea family. The tree usually blooms in late March or April, before its kidney-shaped leaves sprout, and its limbs practically disappear in a cloud of color as its flowers cover branches and sprout from its trunks.

When the striking display of blossoms wanes, pea pods develop. The browned pods often dangle from the trees through the winter. Navajo Indians roast and eat the seedpods.

the red clay trail as the path transits to the benchland between Nasja and Bridge canyons. Tiny yellow flowers speckle the dark sea of **blackbrush** that covers the long bench. **Indian paintbrush** flames occasionally in dark masses of gray-green **blackbrush**. Also, watch for small colonies of **canaigre**. The surrounding rock walls, chewed and smoothed by the elements, help liven up this otherwise scrubby stretch.

Cloistered Oak Canyon at mile 9 has a perennial stream running past several campsites. The narrow gorge is tightly packed with trees and colorful flowers—**western redbud, golden-beard penstemon, western wallflower,** and **western peppergrass**—that hang out near the stream's edge. If you take a short walk up-canyon, you can see where beavers have gnawed cottonwood trees and constructed a dam. On the way out of the canyon, watch for **cliff rock cress.**

After the trail makes its long, rugged descent into Bridge Canyon, look for mounds of **purple vetch** near streamcrossings on the canyon floor. **Skyrocket, golden-beard penstemon,** and **silver-stem lupine** appear in pockets along the path. **Western redbud** becomes prolific as the canyon twists toward Rainbow Bridge.

In the final stretch of benchland right before the bridge, look for **Townsendia daisy** and **little leaf globemallow** in a carpet of **blackbrush** blooming with tiny yellow flowers, and **sego lily,** which continues to the bridge. When you reach the bridge, take a moment to read a plaque embedded in the cliff wall to the right about the Paiute Indian Nasja, who led Wetherill and a handful of explorers to the bridge. Return the way you came.

Sycamore Rim Trail

Wildflower Hike 6

Yellow pond lilies in a bog.

At the KA Hill Trailhead, one of five trailheads along the trail, a field of **Rocky Mountain iris** immediately surrounds the trail. The iris favors boggy ground, a frequent occurrence along the trail as it alternates between stands of ponderosa pines and sunny meadows. The best time to catch **Rocky Mountain iris** in bloom is mid-May.

At mile 0.5, the trail passes a sawmill site that operated from 1910 to 1920. Look down a chasm opposite the site for **mountain ninebark** growing in its preferred habitat of lava flows, **mullein**, and more **Rocky Mountain iris**. Within a short distance, the trail saddles up to Dow Springs, a water stop along the historic 85-mile Overland Road.

Trail Rating	Moderate
Trail Length	11-mile loop
Location	Williams
Elevation	6,500–7,280 feet
Contact	Kaibab National Forest, Williams Ranger District, 928-635-5600
Bloom Season	May–August
Peak Bloom	May and August
Directions	From Flagstaff, take I-40 west about 28 miles to Garland Prairie Road (Exit 167). Exit and go left (south) onto FR 141; continue 8.6 miles and turn right (southeast) on FR 56. Drive 1.7 miles to the trailhead.

Fendler rose, Richardson's geranium, and **wild geranium** gather along the trail as it descends to a string of ponds. If you're hiking this trail during the summer, **yellow pond lily** will beam from the water's surface. Even before the bright yellow blossoms open, you can recognize the plant by its arrow-shaped leaves on the water's surface. On the climb out of the chasm, watch out for **poison ivy** in the rubble of volcanic rock.

Wright's deervetch waits on the rim and follows for most of the rest of the trail. **Yellow columbine** and **creeping barberry** gather near the ruins of a small log cabin, the only remains of the Dow Springs settlement. When the trail dips down into the chasm again, look for **prairie smoke**. The pink bell-shaped flowers turn upward after fertilization and seeds appear on reddish silky plumes that give the plant its common name. **Prairie smoke** is a browse for sheep, whose bells you might hear tinkling in the distance. Sheep herding, rather than cattle ranching, is the tradition in this area.

As the trail parallels the edge of Sycamore Canyon, staying high and dry for several miles, **Indian paintbrush, fine-leaf woollywhite**, Woodhouse's phlox, and **antelope horns** make common appearances along the path. **Claret cup cactus** and **cliff rose** straddle the rim of the canyon. **New Mexico locust** appears where the trail separates from the canyon to cross a drainage. Before the trail reaches the drainage bottom, watch for **birdsfoot lotus**.

The canyon returns to the trail at about mile 4.4. **Cinquefoil** spreads along the trailsides, and **Parry's agave** pokes its yellow clusters up to 18 feet in the air.

At mile 4.5, the Sycamore Vista Point shows a scenic view of the canyon, which has dug deep enough to expose blushing sandstone walls. **Cliff rose** takes its spot along the rim, and **Indian paintbrush** creates its own strata of red color.

At mile 5.5, you'll see Sycamore Falls, an exceptionally scenic gorge where, during snowmelt, a spectacular waterfall pours. The smooth perpendicular wall attracts technical rock climbers. On most summer days you can watch these climbers, who look diminutive from this vantage, make their way up the wall. Stand on the edge of the canyon to see a stand of aspen that found a microclimate conducive to growth.

The trail parts company with the canyon and heads into a pine forest. Watch how **sego lily** appears at a whim in sunny pockets. **Wild chrysanthemum** and **skyrocket** line up along the dapples of sun.

The trail drops into a drainage at about mile 6.5. **Nodding onion** makes its presence known with its mild onion smell. **Rocky Mountain iris, Fendler rose, canyon grape,** and **poison ivy** brush against the trail as it steps gingerly on slate-blue stones in the boggy area.

Once out of the drainage, the trail quickly drops into Pomeroy Tanks, a gathering of natural reservoirs nestled between jagged stone walls. A geological quirk, along with the other ponds and bogs along the trail, the tanks somehow pool in limestone and basalt, which generally drain water. Their oasislike verdancy is jeweled with **Rocky Mountain iris, Fendler rose,** and **groundsel.** Look for **yellow pond lily** in the tanks and **prairie smoke** to return along the trail.

The trail starts its gradual climb up KA Hill with **skyrocket, golden-beard**

YELLOW POND LILY
Nuphar polysepalum

Floating like so many yellow lanterns on the surface of a pond, the yellow pond lily creates a pleasing sight. Usually its arrow-shaped leaves cover the water's surface. A thick network of scaly roots grope along the bottom of the pond. The presence of these lilies in a pond indicates deep water. The lily blooms during the summer months.

Indians roasted the lily's big seeds and ate them like popcorn.

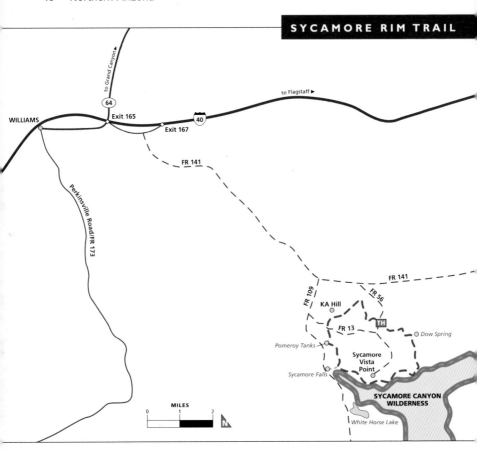

penstemon, and **red-root buckwheat** following on the trailsides. A colony of **Hill's lupine** spreads in a meadow at about mile 9. As the trail climbs in the shade of ponderosa pines, **wild geranium** and **mountain parsley** mix along the path.

By mile 10, the trail tops out at 7,280 feet where you'll get views of Garland Prairie and the San Francisco Peaks. From there, it's another mile back to the trailhead.

Kendrick Mountain Trail

*Wildflower
Hike 7*

*The Kendrick
Mountain Trail
has great views
and a variety
of wildflowers.*

In May 2000, a bolt of lightning kindled a fire on Kendrick Peak's southwest slope. The fire burned 15,000 acres on the mountain. The Forest Service named it the Pumpkin Fire for nearby Pumpkin Center, where early pioneers grew pumpkins.

The fire burned a mosaic pattern up the mountainside. Unnaturally thick from years of fire suppression and grazing, the dense forest burned hot enough to produce 200-foot flames. The coolest part of the fire stayed near the Kendrick Mountain Trail. Firefighters saved the historic cabin near the mountaintop and the trailhead facilities.

Trail Rating	Moderate
Trail Length	4.5 miles one way
Location	Flagstaff
Elevation	8,000–10,400 feet
Contact	Kaibab National Forest, Williams Ranger District, 928-635-5600
Bloom Season	July–September
Peak Bloom	August
Directions	From Flagstaff, drive north about 16 miles on US 180, and turn left (west) onto FR 193. Drive 3.1 miles, and turn right (northwest) onto FR 171; drive about 2 miles and turn right (north) onto FR 190 and drive 0.5 mile to the trailhead.

In the aftermath of the Pumpkin Fire, aspen trees are starting to replace the burned pine trees, and more wildflowers appear in the cooler parts of the burn area. Wildflowers grow well in burn areas because the fires add nutrients to the soil and open up areas to more sunshine. Also, many wildflowers like disturbed areas for seed germination.

The trail starts a nonstop climb to Kendrick Peak in a section of pine forest saved from the fire. **Wild chrysanthemum, mullein,** and **wild geranium** make spotty appearances. **Lambert's locoweed, skyrocket,** and **pink windmill** gather in small clearings. As you climb the slope, you can see the effects of erosion where natural drainages have been eroded by precipitation washing down the barren mountainside.

A large clearing at about mile 0.5 contains a hodgepodge of wildflowers. **Silver-stem lupine** colonizes the clearing with its deep-blue pea blossoms. **Wheeler thistle** sends up tall pink filaments of flowers, and **skyrocket** beams tall orange clusters. **Wandbloom penstemon, spreading four o'clock,** and **Lambert's locoweed** leave hues of purple. These flowers are typical to the many clearings along the trail.

About mile 0.75, as the trail bends west, a gathering of **Wheeler thistle, skyrocket,** and **Lambert's locoweed** color a clearing. This clearing also opens up southern views of the jigsaw flow of meadows surrounded by forests in the countryside below the mountain. A thread of wildflowers weaves along the trail as it starts a series of switchbacks. **Silver-stem lupine, pink windmill, golden-beard penstemon,** and **wild chrysanthemum** make constant companions.

A basalt outcropping at about mile 1.2 turns into a rock garden when the trailside flowers join **western blue flax** and **spreading four o'clock** on the rock. This rocky characteristic strengthens as the trail climbs, showing bouldered bedrock on the upslope. Watch for two borage family members—**bristly hiddenflower** and **many-flowered gromwell**—in the typical trailside mix along this section.

At about mile 1.8, **stemless evening primrose** scatters up the ruddy gravel slopes along the trail like so many discarded tissues. Its night-blooming white blossom has a sweet, musky smell that attracts hawkmoths. The blossom turns pink as it wilts during the day, and the fragrance wanes. **Skyrocket,** with their red tube flowers, are a stunning contrast against the charred logs.

The trail transitions into a mixed conifer and aspen forest at about mile 2. A line of **large-flowered brickellbush** nods frayed rayless flower heads along the trailsides. The trail meanders in and out of the burn area as it continues to climb the mountain and the wildflowers adapt to the trailside shadows. **Arizona rose** and **Indian paintbrush** gather around aspens; **Lambert's loco-weed, wild chrysanthemum,** and **skyrocket** bask in the sunny burn areas. Watch for shows of **golden-eye** and **red-root buckwheat.**

Uninhibited views of the countryside below open up as the

SKYROCKET
Ipomopsis aggregata

The long red tubes of skyrocket flowers make perfect catchments of nectar for humming-birds. The color red immediately draws hummingbirds, while insects and butterflies cannot see red and pass them by. Also, the starburst petals on each flower bend back to prevent insects from resting upon them to take a sip. But the hummingbird's long narrow beak fits neatly into the flower tube as it hovers near the plant.

As pretty as its scarlet blossoms appear, the plant has earned the name skunk flower because it releases a skunky odor from its gland-covered foliage. Nevertheless, pronghorn antelope like to graze the plant. Knowing this, Hopi Indians ground the skyrocket flowers with cornmeal. They presented the meal as an offering before they set out to hunt the animals.

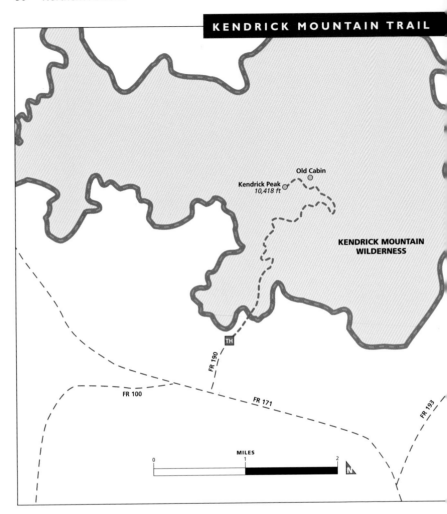

KENDRICK MOUNTAIN TRAIL

Old Cabin

Kendrick Peak
10,418 ft

KENDRICK MOUNTAIN
WILDERNESS

TH

FR 190

FR 100

FR 171

FR 193

MILES

0   1   2

trail zigzags up the mountain. The switchbacks get tighter the higher the trail climbs.

At mile 3, a wave of **bracken fern** covers the slope. Occasional jolts of red from **skyrocket** and **golden-beard penstemon** color the emerald blanket. The trail switchbacks through the ferns, then continues to the east side of the mountain where it presents a telling view of the Pumpkin Fire's path. **Skyrocket** tinges the trailsides orange.

The trail continues to plod upward and around the mountain. Look for **bergamot** and **Whipple's penstemon** growing on an outcropping at about mile 3.3. **Indian paintbrush** cascades from niches in the rock. **Bergamot** follows the trail until it breaks from switchbacking and rounds the mountain into a crowd of **aspen fleabane. Whipple's penstemon** appears on another outcropping along the trail at about mile 3.5.

The trail starts to switchback again, and when it heads west you can see a fire lookout tower. **Groundsel** and **aspen fleabane** cover the clearings along the trail. **Green gentian** prefers the shade.

The trail levels out in a meadow at about mile 4. An old firewatcher's cabin stands in the back of the meadow surrounded by a ring of spruce. Continue west on the trail to hike to the lookout tower.

When the trail starts the last of its switchbacks, watch for **sandwort** and **plains beebalm. Currant** bushes show their ripening fruit. At the rocky mountaintop, just below the lookout tower, **Whipple's penstemon** nestles in rocky niches. Return the way you came.

Red-root buckwheat

Inner Basin Trail

Soothing aspen forests, a meadow full of wildflowers, and montane backdrops make the Inner Basin Trail a favorite summer hike.

Trail Rating	Moderate
Trail Length	2—3.5 miles one way
Location	Flagstaff
Elevation	8,600—10,000 feet
Contact	Coconino National Forest, Peaks Ranger District, 928-526-0866
Bloom Season	July—September
Peak Bloom	Mid-July—mid-August
Special Considerations	Camping, horses, and dogs are not allowed in the Inner Basin in order to prevent contamination of Flagstaff's water supply.
Directions	From Flagstaff, drive north on US 89 17 miles and turn left (west) onto FR 420 (across from the Sunset Crater turnoff, FR 545). Go 0.2 mile and turn right (north) onto FR 552. Drive 1.5 miles to a sign for Lockett Meadow. Bear right (north) and drive another 1.5 miles southwest to the trailhead.

The Inner Basin Trail takes you into a meadow that was the heart of an extinct volcano. The once 15,000-foot-high mountain shattered when it erupted millions of years ago, just as Mount St. Helens did in 1980.

The San Francisco Peaks' highest mountaintops—Doyle, Fremont, Agassiz, and Humphreys—make up the caldera of the volcano, which rings the meadow. Snowmelt from the peaks and summer monsoon rains drain into the basin and its several springs, making it a prime habitat for wildflowers.

The trail climbs a primitive road to the Inner Basin, passing through a stand of aspen trees and mixed conifers. **Silver-stem lupine** makes an impressive display, its pea-flower clusters spreading a blue hue across the forest of silvery-trunked aspen. **Golden-beard penstemon** and **Indian paintbrush** produce attractive red bursts of color. In an especially thick stand of aspen, **Richardson's geranium** spreads across the forest floor.

At mile 1, a sunny hillside draws **sneezeweed**, and **silver-stem lupine** increases. **Golden-beard penstemon** and **bergamot** run up the hillside and follow the trail until it ducks into the shade of mixed conifers.

A series of buildings that belong to the city of Flagstaff, which has its water repository at the basin, will signal that you are almost to the basin. **Red-osier dogwood** and **red elderberry** bushes fill a drainage on the right side of the trail, and **fleabane** covers the shadowed trailsides.

RED ELDERBERRY
Sambucus racemosa

The clusters of red berries on the red elderberry bush will immediately draw your attention as you near this medium-sized bush, unless you hike in early summer. Then the fragrance of its white clusters of flowers may draw you instead.

As eye-catching as this species' flowers and berries are, they are poisonous and you should not consume them in any form. If you want to sample the fruit of an elderberry bush, try its cousin, *Sambucus glauca,* or blueberry elder. These elderberry bushes grow up to 20 feet high, have yellowish clusters of flowers, and produce blue berries. Deer browse the foliage, birds eat the berries, and herbalists use the flowers to break fevers.

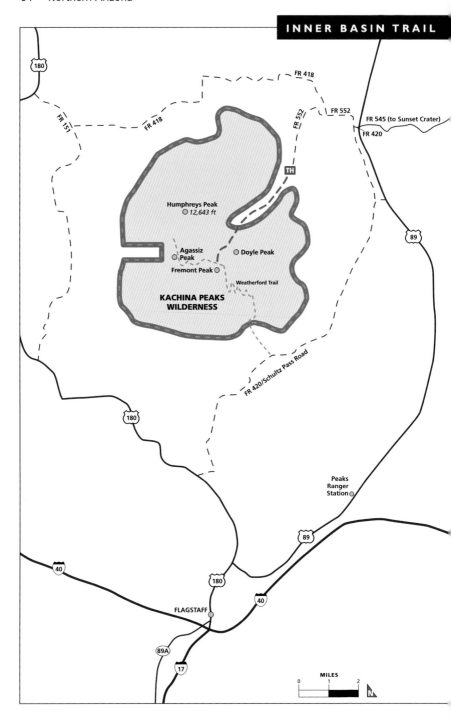

INNER BASIN TRAIL

180

FR 418

FR 151

FR 418

FR 552

FR 552

FR 545 (to Sunset Crater)

FR 420

TH

89

Humphreys Peak
12,643 ft

Agassiz
Peak

Doyle Peak

Fremont Peak

Weatherford Trail

**KACHINA PEAKS
WILDERNESS**

FR 420/Schultz Pass Road

180

Peaks
Ranger
Station

89

40

180

40

FLAGSTAFF

89A

17

MILES
0   1   2

N

A bit farther, **bergamot** and **twinberry** prefer the sunny slope around which the trail bends.

As the trail edges up to the Inner Basin, it enters into full sun. **Fireweed** covers the upslope alongside the trail. This striking magenta wildflower likes disturbed spots in cool areas. It often appears in burn areas, which explains its common name. **Franciscan bluebell** droops light-blue bell flowers along the bottom of the slope. **Richardson's geranium** spreads a lacy trailside cover.

Red raspberry bushes, which like to hang out near water, line the other side of the road where a drainage harbors **red-osier dogwood**. In the spring, the **dogwood** blooms small white flower clusters that produce blue-tinged white berries by August. **Yarrow, sneezeweed,** and **golden-beard penstemon** spread in the strip of land between the drainage and the road.

From the Inner Basin, the trail climbs another 1.5 miles through the meadow and into a forest to the Weatherford Trail. You may finish the trail, or stay in the basin and explore its rich collection of wildflowers. When you're done, return the way you came.

*Wildflower
Hike 9*

Abineau Trail

Colorful slopes around the Abineau Trail.

Trail Rating	Strenuous
Trail Length	2.5 miles one way
Location	Flagstaff
Elevation	8,500—10,400 feet
Contact	Coconino National Forest, Peaks Ranger District, 928-526-0866
Bloom Season	July—September
Peak Bloom	Mid-July—mid-August
Directions	From Flagstaff, drive north on US 89 17 miles and turn left (west) onto FR 420 (across from the Sunset Crater turnoff, FR 545). Go 0.2 mile and turn right (north) onto FR 552. Drive 1.3 miles to FR 418 and turn right (north). Drive 7.6 miles (the road will eventually head west) to FR 9123J and turn left (south). Go 0.7 mile to the trailhead.

The forested slopes on the north side of the San Francisco Peaks contain a cloistered world where botanicals favor moist shadows and sun-loving wildflowers are relegated to small pockets. The Abineau Trail starts and ends in sunny meadows, with most of the trail climbing up shady Abineau Canyon next to a drainage.

While both of the meadows have spreads of wildflowers, the varieties of flowers differ tremendously. The trailhead meadow, teetering between the Transition and Canadian zones, attracts wildflowers comfortable in pine parks.

The meadow at the trail's end lies in the Canadian zone and attracts a different cast of flowers, including some alpine flowers. Though Transition zone wildflowers feel comfortable in the upper meadow, harsh weather conditions may stunt them.

Before you step onto the spur trail between the parking area and Abineau Trail, watch how **butter and eggs**, a butter-yellow snapdragon family member with an egg yolk-colored palette, rings the parking area with **Hill's lupine** and **yarrow**. After only a few steps on the spur trail, inch-high **pussytoes** spread silvery pools.

As the trail enters its first meadow, **silver-stem lupine, mountain parsley,** and **aspen fleabane** spread across the landscape; **Lambert's locoweed** edges the path. Surrounding stands of pines attract **meadow rue** in their shadows.

Large colonies of **thermopsis** and **Richardson's geranium** fill the meadow, often gathering along the trail. When in bloom, the lupinelike **thermopsis** produces clusters of yellow pea blossoms. The early bloomers display fruit pods at the height of the wildflower season.

At mile 0.5, a spread of **Richardson's geranium, purple vetch,** and **fleabane** gathers around a trail sign pointing to the Abineau and Bear Jaw trails. Turn right to continue on the Abineau Trail.

GREEN PYROLA
Pyrola chlorantha

Green pyrola gets its name from *pyrus,* meaning pear tree, because its leaves look like those of a pear tree. Green pyrola's leaves stay green through the winter, and the plant often tenaciously hangs on to the seeds its greenish bell flowers develop along its foot-high stem.

Some Navajo Indians use the green pyrola in a mixture to make a red-colored ceremonial paint.

The trail begins a steep climb up the backside of the mountain in Abineau Canyon. The thick stands of mixed conifers and aspens stuffed inside the narrow canyon give it a dark, mysterious feel, but the trail often gets a bright dose of sunshine in small clearings. The dark earth path, scattered with pinecones and charcoal-gray lava cobbles, looks painted with dabs of yellow from **yellow columbine** and reddish streaks from **woodland pinedrops**. White **Canada violet** and **Richardson's geranium** scatter along the path.

Near mile 1, **currant** and **red elderberry** bushes may display red berries. **Sweet Cicely** gathers in shady spots, revealing tiny green-tinged flowers. You can recognize **sweet Cicely** even when it's not in flower. The leaves resemble those from the parsley family, to which the plant belongs. Its root has an anise flavor, and you can also smell a licorice aroma when you crush the plant's leaves.

TWINBERRY
Lonicera involucrata

Member of the honeysuckle family, twinberry also goes by the name of bearberry honeysuckle. The shrub's black berries make attractive bear food if the birds don't snatch them first.

Twinberry grows in high elevations, especially near streams where it gathers in thickets. Pairs of aromatic yellow tube flowers appear in early summer. If you look closely, you can see how one of the pair's flowers has a short pistil and long stamens; the other has a tall pistil and short stamens. This design allows the flower with long stamens to fertilize its partner's tall pistil.

The canyon widens enough to allow more sunlight at about mile 1.8 and more wildflowers start to show up around the trail. The yellow-orange daisy blossoms of **sneezeweed** gather around the drainage and **Whipple's penstemon** nestles in rocky patches. **Baneberry** bushes show bright red berries, and stalks of **green gentian** rise between the trail and the drainage. Common juniper bushes grow on the slopes of the canyon.

The trail leaves the cover of the forest by mile 2.1, and continues next to the sun-drenched, boulder-strewn drainage. This drainage, which receives snowmelt from Arizona's highest peaks, attracts a rich display of wildflowers.

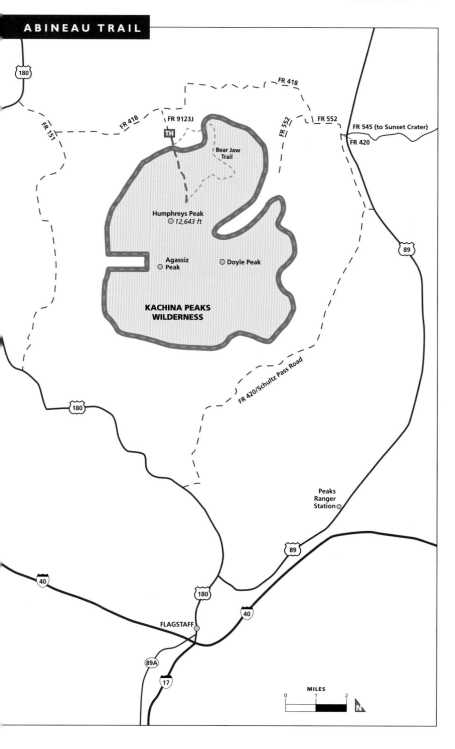

Twinberry bushes show yellow tube flowers in June that develop into twin pea-sized fruit by August. Colonies of **bergamot** lay light purple blankets along the trailside. **Goldenrod** and **cinquefoil** mix with **golden-beard penstemon.**

The trail picks through the stream course for the last 0.25 mile, passing magenta blossoms on **Parry's primrose** tucked into trailside niches. The path ends up in an alpine meadow surrounded by Arizona's tallest peaks.

Sneezeweed spreads up grassy crevices between the mountain peaks and clusters in the mountain meadow. **Fireweed** displays rose-colored flowers that draw your attention wherever they spring up. **Cinquefoil, bergamot,** and **Franciscan bluebell** gather along the meadow's edges.

Take a moment to peruse the slope along an old road at the trail's end. Among its colorful collection of flowers, you may see **Wright's bluets, Whipple's penstemon, green pyrola, twinberry, golden-beard penstemon,** and **yellow columbine.** Return the way you came.

Blankets of wildflowers color a sunny, alpine meadow.

Sandy's Canyon Trail

A cozy slip through an aspen-packed canyon is part of this trail.

Sandy's Canyon, once a wildlife path, gives you an interesting geologic perspective of the Colorado Plateau, at times mirroring shades of the Grand Canyon. The trail was named for Sandy Hartman, owner of the local Hitching Post Stable. In the 1970s, Hartman used to love riding the wildlife path privately, and never took guided tours into the canyon.

By the 1980s, local residents had learned of the place and started using it. The Forest Service then made it part of the trail system. As you hike the trail, you can see why Hartman kept it to herself. The trail skirts the rim of Walnut Canyon, past an anomalous lava flow, then digs into the canyon's limestone walls down to red-hued sandstone walls

Trail Rating	Easy
Trail Length	1.5 miles one way
Location	Flagstaff
Elevation	6,650–6,800 feet
Contact	Coconino National Forest, Mormon Lake Ranger District, 928-774-1147
Bloom Season	July–September
Peak Bloom	August
Directions	From Flagstaff, drive south on I-17 to Lake Mary Road (Exit 339). Drive southeast 5 miles; turn left just after a cattleguard into a day use area; drive to the end of the parking area to the trailhead.

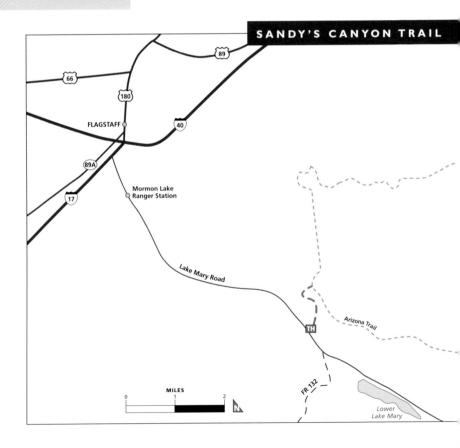

SANDY'S CANYON TRAIL

89

66

180

FLAGSTAFF

40

89A

17

Mormon Lake
Ranger Station

Lake Mary Road

Arizona Trail

TH

FR 132

MILES

0   1   2

Lower
Lake Mary

towards Walnut Canyon. Spreads of wildflowers color meadows and line the forested sections of the path.

The trail starts in a field full of over two dozen different wildflowers such as **poison milkweed, spreading four o'clock, little leaf globemallow, New Mexico vervain, western peppergrass, prairie sunflower,** and **Hooker's evening primrose.** Mixed among them you may see colonies of yellow and white sweet clovers as well.

At the end of the meadow, turn left for the Sandy's Canyon Trail. A right turn will take you to a popular rock climbing area. If you walk to the edge of the canyon, you might see rock climbers on the north wall of the canyon.

Wright's deervetch, butter and eggs, and **goldenrod** follow as the trail leaves the field and ventures out into an open forest of ponderosa pines near the rim of the canyon. As the trail narrows to a single track, look for **amber lily.** This pretty yellow-orange lily with dime-sized star blossoms is the only one of its species that appears in the West.

A colony of coral-colored **Indian paintbrush** gathers in a small clearing. Take a moment at the edge of the canyon rim to look down at the dramatic avalanches of volcanic rock that have tumbled into the canyon. The white bark of aspen trees among the rubble makes a stunning contrast against the porous midnight-black rock.

At a large meadow, mile 0.5, observe the variety

ROCKY MOUNTAIN IRIS
Iris missouriensis

If you see a patch of Rocky Mountain iris along the trail, you can usually count on soggy ground conditions. This native iris likes to get its feet wet, and grows where water gathers.

The Greek goddess Iris inspired the flower's scientific name, which is Greek for rainbow. The Greeks thought the rainbow embodied all of Iris' beauty and represented her role as messenger between the gods and men. They also saw the rainbow as a bridge between the earth and another life.

The rootstock of the Rocky Mountain iris contains a powerful poison called irisin. Warrior Indians used the ground root in a concoction to poison arrowheads. Orrisroot, the ground root of one species of iris, is used as a fixative for potpourri.

of flowers, especially the predominant colonies of **skyrocket**. Veer right to drop into Sandy's Canyon. As the trail descends, **wild geranium** gathers by its side. **Poison ivy** does, too, and the irritating leaves sometimes trespass onto the trail.

The environment becomes cozy as the trail slowly descends the narrow gorge of Sandy's Canyon. **Rockmat** drapes over outcroppings that push toward the trail, **canyon grape** clings to trees and bushes, and colonies of **Arizona rose** and **meadow rue** appear. **Red-osier dogwood** packs into a gulch along the trail.

Once on the canyon bottom, **red cinquefoil** grows among blades of **Rocky Mountain iris**. Iris like to stand near, and sometimes in, water, and they often gather in lowlands where precipitation collects. Clumps of them on dry ground indicate the area has its boggy moments.

The trail makes a quick climb out of the lowland area and comes to a fork. Veer left and follow the trail through an open ponderosa forest. When aspen reappear, another indication of moisture, watch for **hop vine**, which tends toward moist areas, especially around streambanks.

As the canyon widens, the aspen disappear, but ruddy sandstone walls poke through the pines. The trail ends at its intersection with the Arizona Trail. You may continue on the Arizona Trail, or return the way you came.

Walnut Canyon Overlook: Arizona Trail

This section of the Arizona Trail will guide you past dozens of wildflower species.

This hike takes you on a segment of the 790-mile Arizona Trail that covers several distinctive environments on the Colorado Plateau, each one catering to different types of wildflowers. From ponderosa pine meadows to mixed conifer forests, and high-desert canyon in between, this hike gives you a glimpse of the environmental diversity to be found in this relatively small area of Arizona.

The trail ends at the Walnut Canyon Overlook, peering down from pine-covered limestone walls into a unique habitat. Rich in archaeological history, the canyon also has an abundance of botanicals and wildlife.

Trail Rating	Moderate
Trail Length	2.25 miles one way
Location	Flagstaff
Elevation	6,700–6,800 feet
Contact	Coconino National Forest, Mormon Lake Ranger District, 928-774-1147
Bloom Season	July–September
Peak Bloom	August
Directions	From Flagstaff, take I-40 east to Walnut Canyon Road (Exit 204). Go right (south) 2.4 miles (the road becomes FR 622) and turn right (west) onto FR 303; go 1.6 miles to the signed trailhead.

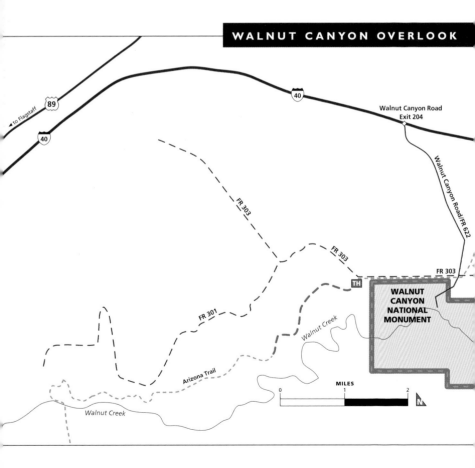

WALNUT CANYON OVERLOOK

The trail starts in a ponderosa park just north of Walnut Canyon. Tall stems of **winged buckwheat** gather along the beginning of the path with **little leaf globemallow, golden aster, and silver-stem lupine. Hill's lupine** scatters down a meadow's mild slope.

The trail heads into the meadow at mile 0.1, providing a look at the yellow snapdragon flowers of **butter and eggs**, purple **wandbloom penstemon,** and pinkish clusters of **red-root buckwheat** that fill the sunny field. **Lambert's locoweed** and **fleabane** edge the trail. Antelope like this type of terrain, and you may see one springing through the meadow.

A showy spread of **silver-stem lupine** stays with the trail until it crosses an unmarked road at about mile 0.4. Watch for **red-dome blanketflower.** The yellow daisy flower has a dome of red disk flowers surrounded by yellow petals.

The bright colors of **wild geranium, Lambert's locoweed, Indian paintbrush**, and **groundsel** make an attractive combination as the trail continues in the meadow. **Thurber's stephanomeria** shows several stages of its purple dime-sized flowers, from bud to feathery bristles. **Many-flowered gilia** sprawls with small purple flowers. Cousin to the red-orange **skyrocket** that is pollinated by hummingbirds, this small gilia attracts bumblebees.

A colony of **cliff rose** appears in a clearing west of the trail at about mile 1. The yellow-petaled blossoms add a distinctive sweet smell to the air until the trail bends west and begins its descent toward Walnut Canyon, about mile 1.1.

A different mix of flowers appears along the trail as it transitions into yet another environment. **Many-flowered**

FERNBUSH
Chamaebatiaria millefolium

Fernbush hangs out on rocky slopes with piñon and juniper trees, and the unobtrusive plant blends well with its environment. The bush's bland sage color might cause you to overlook the plant. But when you stop to take a look at fernbush, you see very distinctive features.

As its common name implies, fernbush has fern-shaped leaves. Its lackluster clusters of white flowers look like its fellow members of the rose family, but have crinkled petals. The plant is sticky. And its sweet scent, which gives the bush its alternate name of desert sweet, doesn't waft like some bushes, but becomes noticeable up close, usually after you've handled its stickiness.

gromwell and **golden-beard penstemon** follow the trail as it switchbacks down raspy limestone into a grove of Gambel oaks. Look for **fernbush, large-flowered brickellbush,** and **rockmat** growing on limestone ledges. **Cliff rose** particularly likes this rocky landscape and appears often.

Yellow-flowered buckwheat brightens the buff, cobbled ground as the trail drops deeper into the canyon. **Banana yucca** shows clusters of white waxy flowers in June and July, then potato-sized fruit by August. This succulent plant held a general-store status with Indians and homesteaders who made food, thread, needles, baskets, mats, and soap from various parts of the plant.

The trail continues in the craggy landscape, dropping deeper into the canyon. **Sweet scent** and **golden-beard penstemon** decorate dingy gray limestone boulders. A colony of yellow **phlox** flowers mix with **little leaf globemallow** under a ledge lined with **Engelmann's prickly pear** cactus at about mile 1.4.

As soon as the trail drops into a drainage and enters a mixed conifer forest at about mile 1.6, **verileaf phacelia, aspen fleabane,** and **meadow rue** appear in the suddenly moist environment. **Silver-stem lupine** return to this forested section of trail, and **Arizona peavine** crawls along the shady path. **Wright's deervetch, many-flowered gromwell,** and **narrow-leaf penstemon** climb out of the drainage with the trail.

Back on the plateau again, the trail weaves in and out of ponderosa pines, past a meadow full of **butter and eggs** and **mullein,** then turns left at about mile 2 to finish at the Walnut Canyon Overlook. **Many-flowered gilia, golden aster,** and **narrow-leaf penstemon** color the trailsides all the way to the Overlook. Return the way you came.

Fisher Point: Arizona Trail

The meadows along Fisher Point are bejeweled with many colorful wildflower gems.

Moderate	*Trail Rating*
1.5 miles one way	*Trail Length*
Flagstaff	*Location*
6,650–7,000 feet	*Elevation*
Coconino National Forest, Mormon Lake Ranger District, 928-774-1147	*Contact*
July–September	*Bloom Season*
August	*Peak Bloom*
High-clearance vehicles are required.	*Special Considerations*
From Flagstaff, take I-40 east to Walnut Canyon Road (Exit 204). Go right (south) 2.4 miles (the road becomes FR 622) and turn right (west) onto FR 303; drive 3.6 miles to FR 301, and turn left (southwest); stay on FR 301 and drive about 4 miles to the trailhead (FR 301 turns sharply north and then south at about 3 miles, see map).	*Directions*

The Arizona Trail at Fisher Point takes you from the ponderosa parks on the Colorado Plateau through a microclimate replicating a higher elevation moist fir-aspen forest as it descends to the west end of Walnut Canyon. Consequently, you get a look at an exceptional mix of wildflowers in a short distance.

The trail starts in a meadow spread with **red-root buckwheat, groundsel, narrow-leaf penstemon,** and **fleabane. Butter and eggs** display two-toned snapdragon flowers on long spindly stems with blue-green leaves. The path,

ROCKMAT
Petrophytum caespitosum

Rockmat doesn't look like it belongs in the rose family, except that the individual flowers in its floral spike have five tiny petals. But its basal spatula-shaped leaves spreading in a three-inch-thick mat on rock walls and boulders don't look anything like the rest of its cousins. Its name, however, fits perfectly: the Greek word *petra* means rock and *phyton* means plant; *caespitosum* means low-growing. You can find rockmat hanging on canyon walls or growing upon shaded boulders.

bending out of the meadow, cuts a corridor through a ponderosa forest. **Lambert's locoweed** and **golden aster** color the clearings. As **Lambert's locoweed** ages, the individual flowers turn from red-purple to light blue. This gives a flattering iridescence to the plant. At a signed intersection, turn right toward Fisher Point.

The trail leads into a colony of **cliff rose** bushes. This rose family member looks similar to its cousin **Apache plume.** However, **cliff rose** grows taller, has fragrant cream or light yellow flowers compared to **Apache plume's** pure white, and has glandular dotted leaves with rounded edges that resemble tiny oak leaves, compared to **Apache plume's** thin downy leaves with no glandular dots.

The mix of flowers at the next signed intersection makes a jewel-toned setting: deep purple **wild geranium, golden aster,** indigo **silver-stem lupine,** and orange **Indian paintbrush.** To continue on this hike, turn right toward Marshall Lake.

Just down the pathway, at about mile 0.5, **mullein** and **goose-foot** gather around a disturbed area by a downed tree. **Goosefoot,** also called lambsquarters, has a drab appearance with tiny green flowers. However, the entire plant turns an

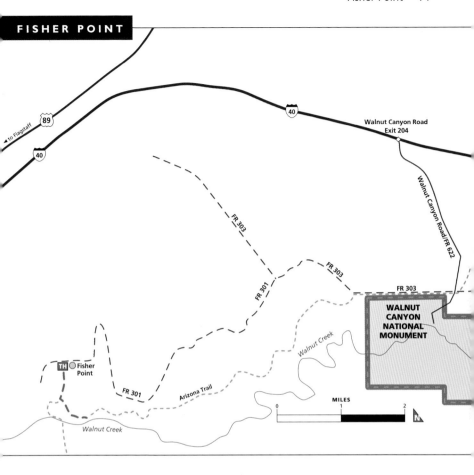

attractive purple in the fall. In spite of its weed status, **goosefoot** rates high in nutrition. The Navajos used it as a staple food.

Butter and eggs spread across the opposite meadow. Also called common toadflax, this bright yellow wildflower has a mouth on its corolla resembling a toad's and its leaves resemble flax. The name refers to the corolla's colors of egg-yolk orange in butter yellow.

Yarrow and **wild chrysanthemum** appear as the trail starts its descent into Walnut Canyon. Watch for clusters of **Wright's bluets** at a rocky clearing where **purple vetch** twines around **skyrocket**. A bit farther, a golden array of flowers gathers on a limestone outcropping: **butter and eggs, golden aster, goldenrod,** and **mullein.** Look also for **sweet scent** in the bunch.

Rockmat lays a green carpet upon the barren patches of rock on the outcropping, looking like a cushion of lichen. **Large-flowered brickellbush** lines the outcropping as it forms into a dingy gray rock wall. **Golden-beard penstemon** growing along the base of the rock wall makes a bold contrast.

The trail starts a series of switchbacks at about mile 0.75. **Silver-stem lupine** covers the trailsides at one switchback, then **narrow-leaf penstemon** and **red-root buckwheat** gather at the next. **Wright's deervetch** lines the path in between with **fine-leaf woollywhite**. **Mullein** and **butter and eggs** partner again in a small meadow. A bit farther, watch for **many-flowered gromwell** and **cinquefoil**.

At about mile 1, the trail twists to parallel itself next to a ravine and enters a moist, forested environment. Lichen hangs from the conifer boughs. **Meadow rue** likes the dampness. **Bergamot** and **large-flowered brickellbush** fill pockets along the path where the conifers allow sun. **Skyrocket** weaves red-orange in the greenness. Look for **butterfly weed** to display showy clusters of orange flowers or upright pods typical to its milkweed heritage.

The trail drops into the ravine next to a colony of **Arizona rose. Sweet clover vetch** tangles in the bushes. You may see **cliff rock cress** growing from dimples in the limestone rock with **large-flowered brickellbush**. **Currant** bushes, which usually bloom in early summer, and **skunkbush**, a springtime bloomer, fill the ravine floor.

When the trail reaches Walnut Canyon, a colorful collection of wildflowers meet on the canyon's sun-drenched floor. Fuzzy **Hill's lupine** fills the mouth of the ravine with **verileaf phacelia, butter and eggs** and **golden-beard penstemon. Spreading four o'clock** and **scarlet gaura** add pink to the mix. Look, too, for the attractive **Rocky Mountain beebalm**. The tall plant's clusters of purple flowers appear down the canyon. Indians used these plants to create paint to decorate pottery.

You may continue on the Arizona Trail, or return the way you came.

Bismarck Lake Trail

The Bismarck Lake Trail travels through open forests and sunny meadows to get to little Bismarck Lake.

Strenuous	*Trail Rating*
1 mile one way	*Trail Length*
Flagstaff	*Location*
8,800–10,400 feet	*Elevation*
Coconino National Forest, Peaks Ranger District, 928-526-0866	*Contact*
July–September	*Bloom Season*
August	*Peak Bloom*
From Flagstaff, drive about 22 miles north on US 180 and turn right (east) onto FR 151; drive 1.6 miles and bear right (south) to continue on FR 151; drive 0.8 mile and turn left onto FR 418B; park.	*Directions*

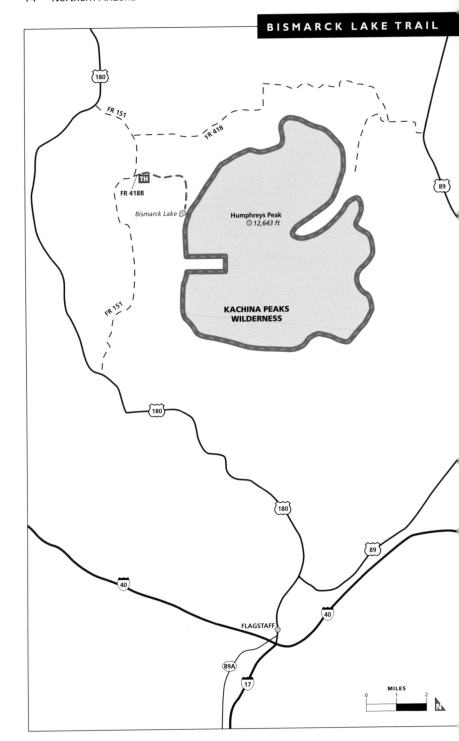

Clinton Hart Merriam, the first chief of the USDA's Division of Economic Ornithology and Mammalogy (an agency that preceded the National Wildlife Research Center), made his base camp along this route to Bismarck Lake around 1889 when he researched the feasibility of his famous life zones theory. Merriam believed that climate gradients produced by elevation and latitude influenced the type of vegetation in an area.

Merriam conducted his research from the desert floor of the Grand Canyon to the tundra mountaintops of the San Francisco Peaks, and came up with six distinct biomes where vegetation types reflected climate changes produced by elevation gains: Lower Sonoran, Upper Sonoran, Transition, Canadian, Hudsonian, and Arctic Alpine. Merriam identified each zone with a major vegetation feature. The zones through which this hike travels, Canadian and Transition, have a predominantly mixed conifer and ponderosa pine forest.

The hike starts in a moist forest environment of mixed conifers and aspen. **Canada violet** spreads like a groundcover along the old road the route follows. The orchid family's **giant rattlesnake plantain** has straight stems from basal leaves, topped with an elongated cluster of tiny white flowers. Except calypso and lady slipper orchids, most orchid family members in Arizona have tiny flowers.

Yellow columbine and **golden-beard penstemon** add

GIANT RATTLESNAKE PLANTAIN
Goodyera oblongifolia

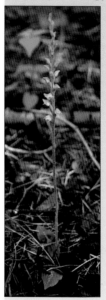

You wouldn't guess the giant rattlesnake plantain belongs to the orchid family. The demure plant pales next to some of its flamboyant cousins.

Orchids have always held an esteemed place in society, to the point of obsession, and at high expense. The orchids' exotic colors and shapes accentuate their mystique and hint at the erotic. Victorian women could not own an orchid plant because orchid flower shapes were "too sexually suggestive for their shy constitution," writes Susan Orlean in *The Orchid Thief.* Even orchids' scientific names intimate their sexual disposition.

In the 19th century, orchid hunters had adventurous lives, often simultaneously playing the part of trailblazer in remote tropical lands. Harvesting thousands of orchids at a time, the collectors frequently ruined forests and plants in the process.

Most of the orchids in Arizona have a lackluster appearance—small green flowers with blushes of red or small white blossoms. The giant rattlesnake plantain fits this description completely. The orchid's small, white, hooded flowers line the flower spike on a leafless stem. The mottled basal leaves of the plant supply its common name because they look like rattlesnake skin.

color to the green environs. **Pinesap** nods cream clusters, and white **Richardson's geranium** speckles the ground, loamy with old aspen leaves and pine needles.

A few steps farther, as the trees allow more sunlight, **Parry's bellflower** mixes in tall grasses with **mountain parsley** and **yarrow**. Cousin to the harebell, **Parry's bellflower** has a more open spread of petals and its leaves are wider. Also, this species has medicinal features. A poultice made from its root treats bruises.

Arizona peavine and **purple vetch** twist in the foliage along the road. Behind the vines, look for **baneberry** and its attractive red berries. **Orange gooseberry** bushes may drip with garnet-colored berries if bears haven't yet eaten them. **New Mexico vervain** fills a sunny clearing on the north side of the road, but **false Solomon's seal** prefers the shadows across the road. During a brief pass through the shadows, **pinesap** likes the rich, moist ground near rotting treefalls. Tiny mushrooms congregate around driplines of pine trees.

Back in the sunshine, **silver-stem lupine** gathers with **golden-beard penstemon** and **Lambert's locoweed**. The **locoweed** has a spice to its scent, similar to carnation. A colony of **sneezeweed** gathers in a circle of aspen on the south side of the road. Watch for **buttercup** in this boggy section.

Veer right at a fork in the road, about mile 0.4, and follow the trail as it cuts through a meadow. **Cinquefoil** and **Hill's lupine** follow the path, and **prostrate vervain** lies right in it. Watch for dandelion-ish **orange agoseris** in the clutter of **Parry's bellflower**, **Lambert's locoweed**, and **wandbloom penstemon**. **Sneezeweed** hangs back by the line of aspen bordering the meadow, and **larkspur** likes the lowland pools.

At about mile 0.5, a plaque in a rock identifies where Merriam stationed his base camp. **Red elderberry** and **orange gooseberry** bushes surround a clearing and **bracted strawberry** lines the path. **Richardson's geranium** and **Brown-eyed Susan** prevail in the spring-fed clearing with ankle-high **heal all**. In about 35 yards, watch for Small Spring and a clearing south of the trail. Turn right on the trail to continue to Bismarck Lake.

The path climbs up a steep ridge through a wooded section where **Canada violet**, **Richardson's geranium**, and **meadow rue** join **bracken fern** in covering the forest floor. **Woodland pinedrops** and **pinesap** love this moist environment. Also look for the light blue clusters of **many-flowered stick seed**.

After a long climb, the trail levels out in the first of a string of meadows separated by stands of conifers. **Silver-stem lupine**, **Indian paintbrush**, and **Lambert's locoweed** color the first meadow. **Yarrow** and **sneezeweed** join up in the next meadow. The third meadow is filled with grass. Dots of color from **cinquefoil**, **Lambert's locoweed**, **wandbloom penstemon**, and **Indian paintbrush** sprinkle across it. Arizona's tallest peaks make a beautiful backdrop in the southeast.

The path crosses a meadow to Bismarck Lake. Return the way you came.

Red Mountain Trail

The high-desert terrain along this trail gathers a nice mix of wildflowers.

The Red Mountain Trail takes you to one of about 600 volcanoes on the San Francisco Lava Field. The surreal amphitheater of orange-tinged volcanic rock at the end of the trail is actually the blown-out side of the volcano, not the vent. The area has eroded into fantasy forms of peaks and spires reminiscent of Bryce Canyon National Park.

The piñon-juniper vegetation zone along the Red Mountain Trail presents an unusual wildflower hike in the high country in several ways. The sun-scorched landscape attracts a different variety of wildflowers than the cool conifer forests in higher country, including flowers that demand less protection from the sun and do well with less consistent moisture levels.

Trail Rating	Easy
Trail Length	1.5 miles one way
Location	Flagstaff
Elevation	6,800–7,000 feet
Contact	Coconino National Forest, Peaks Ranger District, 928-526-0866
Bloom Season	July–September
Peak Bloom	August
Directions	From Flagstaff, drive north on US 180 about 33.2 miles to milepost 247 and turn left (west) onto FR 9023V. Drive 0.3 mile to the trailhead.

Also, the trail is best hiked in the very early morning or late afternoon, for two reasons. First, lower temperatures and less sun intensity produces a safer, more comfortable hike. But these times also give you a look at the night-blooming flowers along the trail; a daytime hike would find them spent or just budding.

The warm, ruddy landscape shows a hint of desolation from the contorted deadfall of juniper trees littering the ground. But the suggestion of elegance from piñon trees mixed with the writhing twist of junipers adds a bit of poetry to the landscape. The whole scene produces an odd coziness. In keeping with the strong elements of the terrain, the wildflowers you find here tend to have bold colors or distinctive features.

The trail starts with colonies of **common snakeweed** and **groundsel** spreading golden across the terrain. **Lambert's locoweed** huddles under piñon trees with a jolt of color from rose-purple elongated clusters. **Pink windmill** wavers on tall spindly stems and **little leaf globemallow** displays rich orange blossoms. The orange-red funnel flowers of **skyrocket** appear arbitrarily, but often, along the trail. The fuzzy palmate plant you see along the trailsides is **Hill's lupine**. Its blue pea flowers bloom around June and July.

As the trail takes you into the thick of the piñon-juniper forest, the scent from the piñon trees oozes like incense. The piñon pine is the most drought-tolerant of Arizona's pine trees, and it produces the popular pine nuts. The one-seeded juniper trees often associate with piñon pines. Large stands of the two trees are called pygmy forests because the piñon and juniper trees grow much shorter than other conifers.

At about mile 0.6, look for **four-winged saltbrush**. The sagelike bush has tiny pale-yellow flowers that mature into seeds encased in paperlike green wing bracts. If you taste the briny leaves of this bush, you'll know why it's called saltbrush. **Bristly hiddenflower** appears in loose clusters.

Colonies of **paperflower** beam with droopy-petaled yellow flowers near mile 0.8. Also, if it's late in the day, look for beautiful pink **wild four o'clock** trailing on the red cinder earth. The large, deep-pink flowers often wait until sunset to open. After blooming, the flowers start to generate a musky odor that will eventually attract its main pollinator, the hawkmoth.

The trail goes into a wash at about mile 1 and follows it. **Cliff rose** forms a corridor painted red with **golden-beard penstemon** and **skyrocket**. **Currant** bushes line the waterway with **bristly hiddenflower** standing at their feet. **Wild geranium** appears when ponderosa pines show up at about mile 1.3.

As the walls of the wash deepen, the pines thicken, creating a dappled path with some relief from the sun. You may notice **bristly hiddenflower** grows larger in the wash than it does on the drier trailside at the beginning of the trail. The wash twines around a handful of ponderosa pines where **meadow rue, pink windmill**, and **wild chrysanthemum** collect.

Cinder slopes rise along the trail, suggesting an aesthetic moonscape. The vegetation that

CLAMMYWEED
Polanisia trachysperma

The numerous gland-tipped hairs on clammyweed's stem provide tactile identification: a wet, sticky feeling when you touch the plant. To add to that curious characteristic, the plant releases an unpleasant smell when you handle it.

Clammyweed's white flowers, however, have pretty features. The four-petaled blooms gush with long pink stamens and are a favorite stop for bees and butterflies. The fruit, upright seedpods, add an unmistakable visual identification to the plant's filamentous flowers.

Clammyweed likes to hang out around sandy washes or roadsides in high desert country.

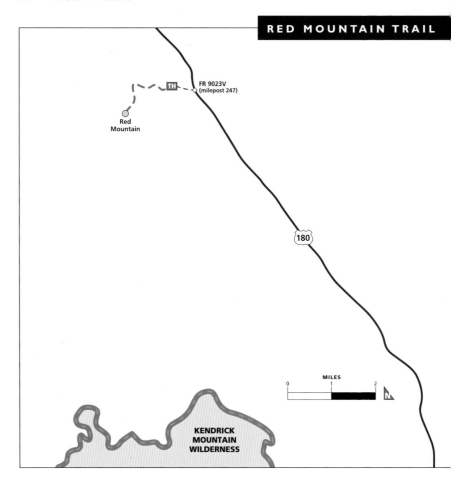

appears sparingly on the slopes produces a dramatic look. Look for **clammy-weed** on the lower part of the sun-drenched northern slope.

Lambert's locoweed leads you to a man-made spillway where a seven-rung ladder lifts you over the wall and onto the volcano. **Taperleaf** bushes stuff themselves into the niches and waterways in the volcano. The bush's name matches its triangular leaves that taper to a tail. The flower's small white buds burst into yellowish rayless clusters. Also called *yerbe de chivato,* or "herb of the he-goat," the plant has a goatlike smell.

When you have finished exploring the volcano, return the way you came.

Slate Mountain Trail

Hikers are escorted by wildflowers along the Slate Mountain Trail.

Slate Mountain, named for its slate formations, rises 1,000 feet above the Colorado Plateau, giving the trail outstanding views of the San Francisco Peaks and surrounding areas. The trail passes from a piñon-juniper forest to mixed conifers with a shift in wildflowers at the turn of the trail.

At the beginning of the trail, as part of the Slate Fire burn area, the subsequent soil conditions have produced a beautiful spread of wildflowers among the charred skeletons of trees. The main outlay of flowers lies in the first 0.5 mile of the trail, but you may want to take the trail to the top to enjoy its spectacular views.

Trail Rating	Easy–moderate
Trail Length	0.5–2.4 miles one way
Location	Flagstaff
Elevation	7,362–8,215 feet
Contact	Coconino National Forest, Peaks Ranger District, 928-526-0866
Bloom Season	July–September
Peak Bloom	August
Directions	From Flagstaff, drive north on US 180 about 25 miles just past milepost 242, and turn left (west) onto FR 191. Drive 1.3 miles and veer right at a fork to stay on FR 191; drive another 0.6 mile to the trailhead.

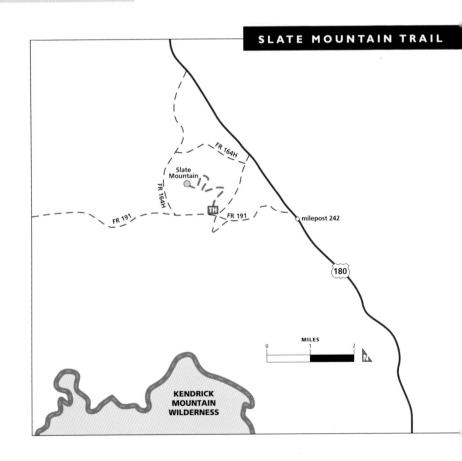

SLATE MOUNTAIN TRAIL

A look around the trailhead will find **two-tone owl's clover, red-root buckwheat, little leaf globemallow,** and **narrow-leaf penstemon** mixed in with charismatic clusters of **Lambert's locoweed** and **goldflower.** The **Lambert's locoweed** and **goldflower** follow you to the trail, then spread in a clearing.

Look for clusters of **white milkwort** atop slender stems. Part of its scientific name comes from the Greek word *polygala,* which means "much milk." **Milkwort** had the reputation of inducing milk production in the cattle that ate the plant. **Pink windmill, Indian paintbrush,** and **many-flowered gilia** add color to the clearing.

Only traces of the burn are noticeable from the clearing. A small burn area off the trail glows with **skyrocket.** But as the trail rounds a bend, it enters the now colorful world of the path of the Slate Fire. **Mullein** feels right at home in the burn because of its propensity for disturbed areas. The showy red flowers of **golden-beard penstemon** look dramatic against the charcoal snags. **Goldflower** continues its golden coverage with purple touches from **wild geranium. Wheeler thistle** converges on the downslope at about mile 0.2.

The trail takes another turn, passing **cliff rose** in the crook of the turn and **bristly hiddenflower** growing across the path from the **cliff rose.** Heading north again, look for **fine-leaf woollywhite** just past four wooden posts. Its odd-shaped yellow blossom tops a leafless stem growing from fernlike basal leaves. **Lambert's locoweed** and **goldflower** continue with the trail as it travels past a line of **cliff rose** in a piñon-juniper community. At mile 0.5, a clearing shows a view of the San Francisco Peaks.

CLIFF ROSE
Cowania mexicana var. *stansburiana*

Navajo Indians call cliff rose "baby diaper." A Navajo mother lines her baby's cradleboard with the diminutive leaves from the cliff rose for their softness, absorbency, and nice smell.

You often find cliff rose, with its leathery wedge-shaped, lobed leaves and shredding red bark, in high-desert canyon country, especially on dry, rocky hillsides. But it can live in elevations as high as 8,000 feet.

The pale-yellow flowers have a potent, but pleasant, fragrance that signals the bush's presence often long before you see it. The bloom season spreads from April to September. The Navajos say October blooms on a cliff rose bush portend deep winter snow.

Banana yucca clusters on the side of the trail. The **yucca's** dramatic cluster of cream-colored bell blossoms bloom early in the spring. By August, it shows its bananalike fruit.

Beyond the view point, the trail proceeds through an exposed route with sporadic wildflower activity in August. Still, a hike through the different vegetation along the path as it climbs to its rocky top in mixed conifers may interest you. Wherever you end your hike, return the way you came.

A fire on the Slate Mountain Trail has created excellent conditions for wildflower growth.

Upper West Fork of Oak Creek

*Wildflowers
climb up red
sandstone walls
on this colorful
and easy hike.*

The West Fork of Oak Creek carves through an extraordinary canyon where Coconino sandstone walls tower hundreds of feet above the crystalline creek. The headwaters of the West Fork of Oak Creek, however, start in a shallow drainage atop the Colorado Plateau. The normally dry drainage packs with wildflowers during the summer.

The wildflowers start as soon as you drop into the drainage from the wooden bridge on FR 231. Family members **Richardson's geranium** and **wild geranium** grow together in clusters. Colonies of **bergamot** lay clusters of purple next to 4-foot-tall stalks of **showy milkweed**.

Trail Rating	Easy
Trail Length	0.5 mile one way
Location	Flagstaff
Elevation	6,490 feet
Contact	Coconino National Forest, Peaks Ranger District, 928-526-0866
Bloom Season	July–September
Peak Bloom	August
Special Considerations	Watch for flash floods
Directions	From Flagstaff, head west on Old Highway 66 and turn left (south) onto Woody Mountain Road (FR 231); drive about 18 miles to the bridge at the West Fork of Oak Creek and park.

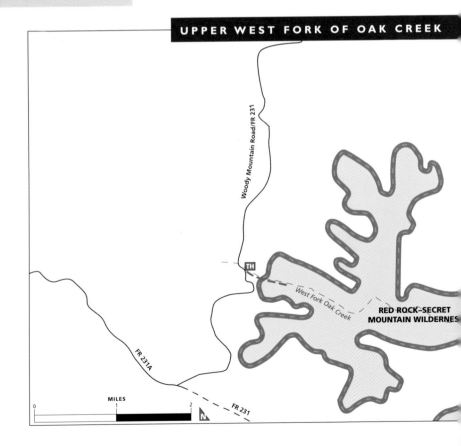

UPPER WEST FORK OF OAK CREEK

Woody Mountain Road/FR 231

TH

West Fork Oak Creek

RED ROCK–SECRET MOUNTAIN WILDERNESS

FR 231A

FR 231

MILES
0   1   2

N

Large-flowered brickellbush hangs frayed-edged blossoms next to pure-white clusters of **yarrow**. As you step into the drainage and weave around willows and **Fendler rose** bushes, watch for **poison ivy**.

Yellow columbine and **meadow rue** like the rainforest environment in the drainage. The moisture encourages lichen to grow. The lichen drips from spruce trees like tinsel on a Christmas tree. **Canyon grape** drapes from pines onto a sandstone out-cropping below. Just across the drainage, a group of **larkspur** plants stand in the midst of a colony of **Fendler rose**. Watch for **New Mexico checkermallow** next to the southern banks of the drainage.

If you arrive in the drainage early enough in the day, you may spot a herd of elk clomping up the slopes into the forest. The drainage provides forage for them. You may see where they've munched the tops of wild-flowers such as **thermopsis, wild chrysanthemum,** and **verileaf phacelia.**

As you hike down the drainage across its rocky floor, **Indian paintbrush** appears on the north slope. On a patch of bedrock, **mullein** and **Nuttall's linanthus** take advantage of some soil that is conducive for rooting. **Goldenrod** mixes with **butter and eggs.**

At about mile 0.25, a footpath forms on a bench on the south side of the drainage. **Western wallflower** sends up shocks of orange

BERGAMOT
Monarda menthaefolia

Named for a Spanish physician and plant collector, Nicolas Monardes, bergamot holds a fascinating place in American history. While the plant's scientific name *Monarda* comes from Monardes, *menthaefolia* means "mint-leaved." The volatile oils in this member of the mint family's leaves produce a strong flavor and scent akin to a species of citrus in Italy called bergamot. These oils contain thymol, an antiseptic.

When colonists started to wrangle free of England's hold, the Boston Tea Party led to a shortage of their favored blend of tea called Earl Gray (a black tea flavored with bergamot oil). Thanks to the Oswego Indians, who introduced the colonists to *Monarda menthaefolia* and taught them how to make a tea from it, the colonists could continue enjoying teatime with the coveted bergamot taste.

clusters along the meadow edges, and **green gentian** gathers below spruce trees. **Bracted strawberry** crawls along the trail edges and **cinquefoil** gathers at its sides. **Winged buckwheat** displays yellow-green blossoms.

The path re-enters the drainage at about mile 0.4. If you are hiking in peak bloom, you may see berries on **red-osier dogwood** bushes. The red-stemmed bushes produce white clusters of flowers in May and June and blue-white berries by August.

Soon the canyon walls draw nearer and the drainage floor narrows at about mile 0.5, provoking a brushier environment with less herbaceous plants. Return the way you came.

Pinesap prefers moist, shady areas in which to grow.

West Fork Trail

Brown-eyed Susan grows along the banks of the West Fork of Oak Creek.

The West Fork of Oak Creek lies in a Research Natural Area, which has many of the general area's best representatives of natural plant communities. This trail has sensitive and rare plant species. The Forest Service requests that hikers keep their groups to 12 or less and stay on the maintained trail to preserve the plants and the soil stabilization and watershed protection of this delicate area.

As soon as you pass the sign identifying the West Fork Trail, you pass from the sere high desert to the lusciousness of a canyon riparian environment. **Himalaya berry** brambles produce plump berries, and **Arizona rose** shows ripe red fruit called hips. Oversized **meadow rue** dangles red-tinged tassels, and **poison ivy** announces its maturity with white berries.

Trail Rating	Easy
Trail Length	3 miles one way
Location	Sedona
Elevation	5,400–5,500 feet
Contact	Coconino National Forest, Sedona Ranger District, 928-282-4119
Bloom Season	July–September
Peak Bloom	Mid-July–mid-August
Special Considerations	The Forest Service charges a $5 parking fee. The trail is located in the Red Rock–Secret Mountain Wilderness where no mechanized vehicles, including mountain bikes, are allowed.
Directions	From Sedona, drive 9.9 miles north on AZ 89A to the Call of the Canyon parking area on the west side of the highway.

A bit farther near the bridge crossing the West Fork of Oak Creek, **horehound** dabbles on the south side of the trail with **white nightshade** and **common mallow**, but colonizes the creekside slope, showing its white clusters of flowers. **Horehound** has a square stem and medicinal properties, typical of the mint family to which it belongs. Like most mints, **horehound** has a calming effect on the body and helps with digestion. An infusion made from its downy wrinkled leaves also helps sooth coughs and hoarseness.

Himalaya berry and **horehound** came to the West Fork of Oak Creek with homesteaders. Both are considered invasive plants and the Forest Service plans to decrease these species to allow native plants a chance to return and re-establish themselves.

As you cross the bridge, the red flower you see congregating along the banks is **cardinal flower**. Once you get to the other side of the bridge, look for **golden aster** and **verileaf phacelia** climbing a man-made rock wall. **Skyrocket** shoots above a spread of **bracken fern**, and **sacred datura** mounds along the red-tinged path that heads toward the ruins of the Mayhew Lodge.

The lodge, which saw the likes of Warren Harding, Clark Gable, and Carole Lombard, no longer stands. But you can see its cellar and storage building on the north side of the trail.

As you pass the trail registry, about mile 0.3, the trail gets brushy. Still, pockets of color appear with **western dayflower**, **bergamot**, and **pink windmill**.

Sunny spots draw **white evening primrose**, but **Canada violet** likes the shade of a line of boxelder trees.

After the first of several creek crossings, **bergamot** and **wild geranium** follow you to the next crossing at mile 0.4. Once across the creek, look for pale-yellow star flowers on **polemonium** in a cover of **canyon grape**. **Wild geranium** grows to twice its size here in its fight for sunlight with **bracken fern**. **Green-flowered macromeria** nods trumpet clusters from a yard-long, hairy-leaved plant. Watch for **larkspur** in a sun-drenched colony of **bracken fern** on the north side of the trail, and more **polemonium** in a shady clearing.

As the path drops down a stairstep of rocks, **large-flowered brickellbush** and **red figwort** cascade on the north slope. **Red-osier dogwood** along the creek-side shows white berries.

Poison ivy makes a big show at the next creek crossing, and mixes in with the **agrimonia**, **Richardson's geranium**, and **monkshood** that stand near the creekbanks. Be careful not to let **poison ivy** brush against exposed skin. Most people have a sensitivity to the plant and end up with an itchy, weepy rash.

Pearly everlasting takes to the upslope as the trail passes a brushy stretch all the way to the next creek crossing at about mile 1. Look for more **green-flowered macromeria** on the trail's north side. Like most of its borage family cousins, **green-flowered macromeria** has a cover of bristly hairs.

A colony of **pearly everlasting** gathers as the trail nears the creek for its fifth crossing. Sometimes it is confused with Arizona cudweed, but you can tell the two apart by their blossoms. **Pearly everlasting** has a more pure white, round flower; Arizona cudweed blooms dingy-yellow rayless flowers.

After a rock-hop across the water, look for more **pearly everlasting** hanging on the showy

PEARLY EVERLASTING
Anaphalis margaritacea

Pearly everlasting is sometimes confused with Arizona cudweed. A major difference between these two members of the sunflower family is that pearly everlasting has a woolly underside to its leaves, which also continues onto its stem, while Arizona cudweed's entire leaf is woolly, as well as its stem.

The two also differ in their flowers. The name *margaritacea* means "pearly." Clusters of pearly-white bracts surround tiny yellow flowers on pearly everlasting. Arizona cudweed has dingy rayless blossoms tipped with tan.

Pearly everlasting's flowers preserve well, which explains their common name. Herbalists make a tea from the plant to treat coughs and colds.

sandstone walls carved, then smoothed, by erosion. **Cardinal flower** and **yellow columbine** color the bank of the creek. Farther on the trail, **Nuttall's linanthus** and **skyrocket** share space with **bracken fern.**

At mile 1.7, the canyon walls close in on the trail, giving the hike an intimate feeling. Mixed conifers climb the red rock walls and walk their ledges. Near the creek, plants grow in cracks and niches. **Hooker's evening primrose** picks in the slabs of sandstone piled along the trail from a landslide. If you see or hear rocks fall during your hike along the West Fork Trail, you're observing the process of erosion. Though unusual to witness, the natural process plays a part in the formation of canyons and their exquisite features.

The trail pulls closer to the creek and the floral displays of **false Solomon's seal, large-flowered brickellbush,** and **polemonium.** At the seventh creek crossing, after passing peppery-tasting **plains beebalm** and pretty **common monkey flower** with its yellow blooms, the trail clatters over a bedrock stretch of the creekbed and winds through a distinctive S-curve in the canyon. Lining both sides of the West Fork Trail is **Richardson's geranium,** along with **bergamot** and **mullein.**

Look for **golden-beard penstemon** to line the creekbank when you make the eighth creek crossing. On the other side, **monkshood,** also called wolfbane (folklore says that it will ward off the evil

SACRED DATURA
Datura meteloides

Mainly a summer bloomer, sacred datura will show its enchanting light mauve trumpet flowers as early as April if the weather is warm enough. One of its alternate names, moon lily, describes the flower's bloom

cycle: the lemon-scented flowers bloom at early evening, then wither as the sun rises.

Moths have an attraction for sweet-smelling white or light-colored flowers like the sacred datura. Pollinators with a long enough proboscis, such as hawkmoths, sip the flower's nectar during the night hours.

Every part of the sacred datura plant is toxic. Even its pollinators become intoxicated with its nectar, flying erratically and falling off the edge of the flower's cup. The hawkmoth's large, green-horned caterpillars (called hornworms) munch on the poisonous plant and become poisonous themselves.

Hopi shamans used the plant to induce visions. Curious people who experiment with the plant will become sick—many seriously —and some will not live to talk about the experience.

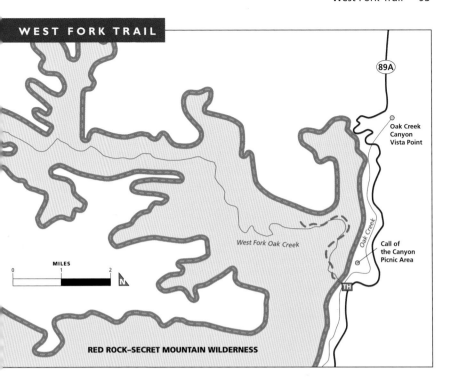

WEST FORK TRAIL

89A

Oak Creek
Canyon
Vista Point

Oak Creek

West Fork Oak Creek

Call of
the Canyon
Picnic Area

TH

MILES
0   1   2

N

RED ROCK–SECRET MOUNTAIN WILDERNESS

werewolf), stands several feet tall in a feeder channel of the creek with **brown-eyed Susan** and **agrimonia.**

A colony of **horsetail** spreads around the trail and follows you across the creek—past the **agrimonia** that likes to hang out on the creekbanks—and along a curl of sandstone in the canyon wall. Also called scouring-rush, **horsetail's** green reeds were used by homesteaders to clean pots. **Canada violet** lines the trail during this shadowy stretch of trail. **Monkshood** gathers next to another curl of sandstone.

The trail drops into the drainage, then makes its last creek crossing. The path climbs high above the creek, brushing up against **large-flowered brickellbush** and **false Solomon's seal,** then drops back into the drainage to its end, where the canyon walls squeeze into the creek and require you to wade.

If you don't mind getting your feet wet, you may wade through the water and continue. An unmaintained trail will take you deeper into the canyon, crossing knee- to thigh-deep water. At mile 5, a chest-deep pool makes a good turnaround point. Return the way you came.

Wildflower Hike 18

Wilson Canyon Trail

Many high-desert flowers bloom on the beautiful redrock slopes of Wilson Canyon.

The Wilson Canyon Trail scrambles through a canyon named after an Arkansas bear hunter, Richard Wilson. Wilson met his match one day in the canyon. A grizzly bear caught Wilson without his trusty bear gun, which was in the shop for repairs, and he merely wounded the bear. The bear turned on him, and Wilson died about a half mile from the canyon's parking area.

The trail starts on an old sunny road along the canyon's rim lined with **sugar sumac** and **point leaf manzanita** bushes. **Sugar sumac** bushes

Trail Rating	Easy
Trail Length	1.5 miles one way
Location	Sedona
Elevation	4,500–5,000 feet
Contact	Coconino National Forest, Sedona Ranger District, 928-282-4119
Bloom Season	March–May
Peak Bloom	April
Special Considerations	A Red Rock Pass fee of $5 is charged for recreation parking. Part of this trail is located in the Red Rock-Secret Mountain Wilderness where no mechanized vehicles, including mountain bikes, are allowed.
Directions	From Sedona, go north on AZ 89A and drive about 1.6 miles to the Midgley Bridge parking lot.

bloom early, usually in March, but **point leaf manzanita** bushes bloom in the heart of the season. **Feather dalea** displays feathery clusters of purple pea flowers that provide its alternate names of indigo bush, pea bush, and feather plume. The foot-high bushes appear often along the trail.

Blackfoot daisy mounds on the upslope along the road with the milkweed family's **antelope horns**. A rainy season will coax **sego lily** to bloom across the slope. Gorgeous clusters of **banana yucca** hang from stalks jutting from bayonet-shaped basal leaves. A colony of **little leaf globemallow** surrounds pretty pink **Palmer's penstemon** next to the rim's edge.

At a sign for the Wilson Canyon Trail, about mile 0.1, continue on the road straight into the canyon; the Wilson Canyon Trail goes to the right and rejoins you further on. As you drop towards the canyon floor, **feather dalea** bushes climb up the terraced red rock slopes; their backlit, feathery blossoms illuminate in the sun, accentuating their scientific name *formosa*, or "beautiful." **Wild parsley's** dirty white umbels edge the road. **Golden-beard penstemon** takes to the downslopes heading into the canyon.

At about mile 0.25, you will pass the ruins of an old redrock bridge, once part of the original road into Oak Creek Canyon. Just beyond the ruins, the trail drops into Wilson Canyon. As soon as it does, look for **cliff rose** on the south side of the wash. **Mountain mahogany** bushes line the floor of the canyon displaying yellow-green tube flowers. **Point leaf manzanita** bushes dangle pink bell flowers along the path.

A pour-off, usually pooled with water, attracts a colony of **false toadflax**. A member of the sandalwood family, **false toadflax** has a parasitic nature, tapping the roots of neighboring plants.

Near the Red Rock–Secret Canyon Wilderness boundary, about mile 0.4, **Utah swertia** likes sun-dappled spots and **Palmer's penstemon** greets you at the wilderness boundary.

The path parallels the creek, climbing up and down gentle rises, and crosses the creek from one side to another. **Locoweed** blooms purple clusters from pale-green mounds of leaves on the north canyonslope at around mile 0.5. The flowers develop into fat seedpods. **Blue Dicks**, a common springtime wildflower in the desert areas, makes an occasional show along with **New Mexico groundsel**, the most common of the groundsels in Arizona. A colony of **star gilia** fills a small rocky clearing. **Miner's lettuce** spreads in depressions on the southern slope where rainwater has pooled.

By about mile 0.6, Wilson Mountain rises in the near distance. A bit farther, the path crosses the drainage past a dryfall that may have threads of water streaming from it. When the trail reaches the canyonslope again, watch for the yellow flower clusters of **Arizona bladderpod**.

Arizona cypress trees squeeze in on the trail at about mile 0.75, and the path flirts with the canyon

BANANA YUCCA

Yucca baccata

The enormous cluster of flowers on banana yucca make an attractive late spring sight, especially when a colony of the plants covers a high desert hillside. The waxy, white three-inch-long flowers practically glow in the sun.

In moonlight, the bell flowers grow even more special. They become a makeshift nursery for the female yucca moth, *Pronuba yuccasella*. The yucca moth, during her egg-laying and nursery-preparation ritual, ends up pollinating the banana yucca.

After the female moth mates, she collects pollen, rolls it into a ball a bit bigger than her head, tucks it under her chin, then flies to another flower where she lays her eggs on its pistil. Then the moth presses the pollen ball on the stigma, pollinating the flower. In a few days, her eggs hatch, and the larvae feed on yucca seeds. Each larva drops to the ground, buries itself, cocoons, then emerges in the spring to unwittingly help pollinate another banana yucca.

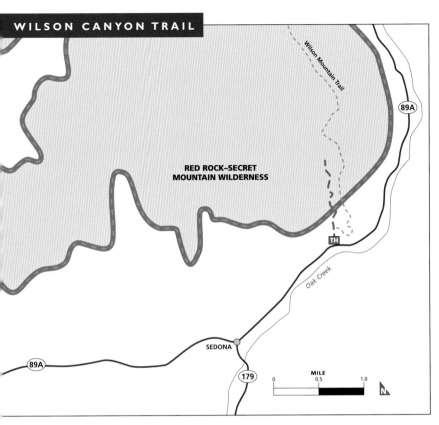

floor, alternately crossing it and walking along it. The trail finally stays put on the floor, and starts scrambling up a bouldered route. **Locoweed** makes a comeback, as well as **cliff rose** bushes. **Indian paintbrush** pretties up the canyon walls with its coral blossoms. Watch, too, for **claret cups** on the walls.

The path ends at a bouldered logjam in the drainage. All around, red and white sandstone mountains create an extraordinary scene. Return the way you came.

*Wildflower
Hike 19* # Barnhardt Trail

*Flannel bushes
bloom along the
Barnhardt Trail.*

The Mazatzal Mountains, one of the more rugged mountain ranges in the state, can take hikers to places where they may not see another person for days and, depending on the trail, maybe weeks. Steep, rocky trails climb razorback ridgelines and high desert vegetation pricks and tears at bodies and clothes, creating the mountains' characteristic austere personality. Nevertheless, the pleasant, inspiring scenery of these mountains offers a comfortable atmosphere, more amicable than hostile.

The range's unusual name experiences some quirky pronunciations. The "proper" pronunciation is Mah-zaht-zal. Arizona's state historian, Marshall Trimble, says many Arizona place names have been wrangled by pronunciation

Trail Rating	Strenuous
Trail Length	3—6.2 miles one way
Location	Phoenix—Mazatzal Wilderness
Elevation	4,200—6,000 feet
Contact	Tonto National Forest, Payson Ranger District, 928-467-3200
Bloom Season	Late March—June
Peak Bloom	April
Special Considerations	High-clearance vehicles are suggested.
Directions	From Shea Boulevard in Phoenix, take AZ 87 north 47.2 miles to the Barnhardt Trail turnoff; turn left (west) on FR 419 and drive 5 miles to the trailhead.

deviations. The locals say Ma-te-zel because the name rolls off the tongue easier. Trimble pronounces the name as his father, who punched cattle in the area, pronounced it: Mah-tah-sail. Nevertheless, Trimble advises to "go with the locals, or it may double the price of your drinks."

For all the difficulties the mountains pose in terrain and name, one of the nicest high desert shows of wildflowers in the spring is along the Barnhardt Trail. A popular trail year round, the Barnhardt Trail also takes hikers through spectacular scenery as it climbs to the head of Barnhardt Canyon.

During the first mile of the trail, colonies of **Coulter's lupine** follow the path as it climbs up sun-touched slopes. **Feather dalea, fleabane**, and **New Mexico groundsel** make common sights. Watch for the deep-orange blossoms on **little leaf globemallow** and the stunning orange **western wallflower.**

An occasional spike of a **golden-flowered agave** may unfurl an early shoot. The flower clusters, however, typically don't bloom until June, looking like so many yellow lanterns beaming on the mountainsides.

Just past the wilderness boundary, you may catch glimpses of Barnhardt Creek several hundred feet below the trail through the line of bushes that start appearing along the path. The white **cliff fendler bush** blossoms have four spoon-shaped petals. Its shiny, dark green leaves, a favorite of deer, have three prominent sunken veins. The Navajo Indians use them in a smoking mixture.

Deerbrush, with its sweet fragrance that gives it the alternate name of white lilac, is also browsed by deer. Indians used the bark to create a soapy mixture, which gives the plant another alternate name: soap bush.

Just below the trail on the downslope, you may notice stunning bursts of yellow-orange flowers from the **flannel bush**. The Mazatzal Mountains provide the spreading bush's favorite habitat of dry slopes and pine forests.

If you hike in March, you may catch the tail end of the **sugar sumac** bush's bloom season and find white clusters tinged pink with buds on the tall bushes. Its leaves sometimes have a maroon blush. Also, depending on the time of your hike, you may see the unobtrusive flowers of the **quinine bush** or the bush's cluster of green fruit.

At about mile 2, rocky ledges have scarlet **claret cup cactus** coloring their edges. Also watch for **rock echeveria** nestled in the outcroppings' nooks. Where piñon pines and oaks provide enough shade, **waterleaf** and **osha** make a surprising show.

By about mile 2.5, the geology of the canyon grows tumultuous. The canyon's north wall shows pressured strata and jagged lifts of maroon cliffs. Trailside, **Indian paintbrush** and **New Mexico groundsel** show bold coral and gold colors.

At about mile 3, the trail climbs to a maroon-colored chasm pouring a stream of water that pools around and across the trail. When the snow melts, a spectacular waterfall cascades down a chute in the back of the chasm. This wet environment supports a variety of moisture-loving flowers.

POISON IVY

Rhus radicans

Attracted to disturbed areas, poison ivy often appears at the edges of trails passing through moist and shady environments. A poisonous resin called urushiol makes the plant the bane of most hikers' existence.

Though some people are more sensitive than others, most will experience a reaction when their skin is exposed to the plant. People often have no sensitivity to the plant on their first encounter with it, but become more sensitive with each subsequent experience. The affected area will start to itch within several hours, and a rash will appear and eventually ooze. This ordeal will usually end within one to four weeks.

Every part of the plant can cause an allergic reaction, from its leaves to its yellowish berries, whether the plant is verdant green or withering. Even inhaling smoke from the plant will cause a rash.

If you brush up against poison ivy, quickly douse the area with cold water and wash with soap if possible. Remember, the best remedy is prevention—*leaves of three, let it be!*

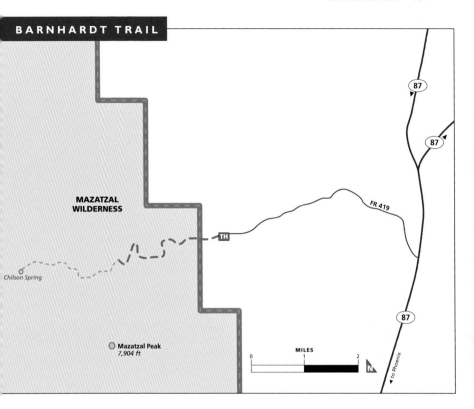

Look for loose clusters of tiny pink flowers on **alumroot** nestled in the ledges on the chasm wall. **Common monkey flower** lines the stream edges with **false toadflax. Yellow columbine** arches from the streamside. Also watch for **poison ivy.** Normally a 1- to 2-foot-tall shrub, **poison ivy** grows much taller in this area.

The chasm makes a good turnaround point, but you may continue to the trail's end at Chilson Spring. Return the way you came.

Wildflower Hike 20

See Canyon Trail

Canyon grape and wildflowers cluster around moist areas near Christopher Creek along the See Canyon Trail.

Trail Rating	Moderate
Trail Length	0.5–3.7 miles one way
Location	Payson
Elevation	6,160–7,860 feet
Contact	Tonto National Forest, Payson Ranger District, 928-474-7900
Bloom Season	July–September
Peak Bloom	August
Directions	From Payson, drive east on AZ 260 about 21 miles to FR 284; turn left (north), and drive 1.6 miles to the trailhead.

Named for Charley and John See, the father and son who settled at See Spring around 1900, the trail is one of the more popular hikes on the Mogollon Rim. A pretty hike that traces Christopher Creek to its start at the Mogollon Rim, the See Canyon Trail produces a lovely show of wildflowers during an active monsoon season.

The trail starts in a pine-hardwood forest, and immediately drops into the Christopher Creek drainage. Dappled and damp, the creeksides harbor colonies of **Arizona rose, meadow rue,** and **agrimonia. Hop vine** crawls on bushes and trees. You may see **horsetail** in its usual form as a sectioned green reed, or sprouting tassels like a horse's tail. The fertile **horsetail** develops jointed branches, while the infertile plant remains a reed.

The trail climbs out of the drainage as quickly as it dropped in. Once out of the drainage, take a moment to study the small clearing about 40 feet to the left. **Skyrocket** sends up red-orange clusters that rub shoulders with **Hooker's evening primrose.** Tender **scarlet gaura** and **pink windmill** have pink flowers on thread-thin stems. **Red cinquefoil's** deep-red flowers look like velvet. Blue **western dayflower** mixes with **Canada violet** and **yarrow.**

As the trail passes another small clearing to the right, watch for **scarlet creeper** and **Gray's lima bean** to mingle with **skyrocket** and **yellow columbine.** At a fork, veer left to continue on the See Canyon Trail. But before you do, look for **green-flowered macromeria.**

Unpretentious, with pale-green flowers, **green-flowered macromeria** is often passed by. The Hopi Indians, however, held the plant in high enough esteem to use it in rainmaking ceremonies.

The trail continues through a wooded section that shelters an emerald array of **bracken fern** and a luxurious growth of grass. This moist environment fosters colonies of **mountain lobelia** intermixed with **Canada violet, verileaf phacelia,** and **yarrow** along the borders of the trail. Take a moment in a clearing on the left, at about mile 0.3, and you may find **large-flowered brickellbush** and **yellow columbine** cascading from a tangle of **canyon grape. Canada violet** and **wild geranium** fill the clearing, while **Hooker's evening primrose** stands back around the edges.

A bit farther on the trail, **thermopsis** melds with **bracken fern** and **cleavers** showing more green than color. Because **thermopsis** (also called golden pea) shows its yellow clusters of pea blossoms in the spring, you only have its large, cloverlike leaves to identify the plant in other seasons. **Cleavers** have tiny white flowers that you may not see at first glance. The trailing plant, also called bedstraw, was used to fill sleeping cushions. **Bracken fern** has no flowers, but is the most prevalent fern in Arizona. You may see **woodland pinedrops,** which like to grow among ferns.

Another clearing along the trail fills with **bracken fern** and **silver-stem lupine**. As the trail continues, waist-high grass forces out **bracken fern**, but **silver-stem lupine** grows to extraordinary heights to grab the sunlight it needs. **Groundsel** adds bright yellow clusters of flowers, and **Wright's deervetch** has a mixture of yellow pea flowers that turn orange when fading. Watch for **many-flowered gilia** along the trail, and **woodland pinedrops** in the ferns.

Arizona rose, ripe with hips, gather around the path at about mile 0.4. Rock patches along the trail collect water in wet weather and **heal all** and **bergamot** scatter around them.

The trail pulls away from the creek at about mile 0.5 and starts its climb toward the top of the Rim. The wildflowers dwindle to **Wright's deervetch, Fendler's hawkweed**, and **New Mexico yellow flax** in this drier environment. This makes a good turn-around point for a short day hike. You may, however, continue on the trail.

At mile 1, the trail passes the intersection with the See Spring Trail, a spur trail just over a half-mile long that leads up to the spring where Charley See settled.

About 0.25 mile farther, the spring trickles across the trail toward Christopher Creek. Look for **Virginia creeper** and **cardinal flower** around its flow. These plants have interesting contrasting features. **Virginia creeper** hardly shows its green-tinged flowers. However, its leaves always make a distinctive show, especially in the fall when they flame red. **Cardinal flower's** toothed leaves, on the other hand, are hardly noticed because of its showy red flowers.

MOUNTAIN LOBELIA
Lobelia anatina

Mountain lobelia's lavender tube blossom looks similar to most species in the lobelia genus: it has two upper lobes and three larger bottom ones. One particular feature of this species is its crossing upper two lobes. This species lives near Arizona's mountain streams or moist meadows.

Another species occurring in Arizona, *Lobelia cardinalis,* or cardinal flower, also has two smaller upper lobes and three larger lower lobes. This flower's particular feature is its cardinal red color, which attracts hummingbirds.

Lobelia inflata, which normally appears east of the Mississippi, is touted by some herbalists as a panacea. But its intense emetic properties have caused poisoning, and the plant should never be used without caution and professional supervision.

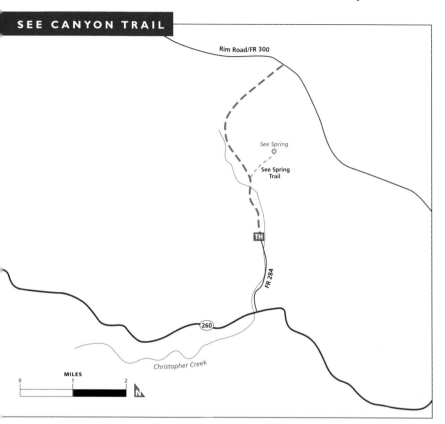

The trail meets up with the creek drainage again, inviting back the moisture-loving wildflowers seen earlier on the trail. **Poison ivy**, at times, becomes prolific, so be careful.

At this point, too, the trail becomes austere in its climb to the top. Trail washouts appear and the grade has intensely steep moments. One particularly confusing washout occurs at mile 2. Cairns will indicate routes on both sides of the drainage. For the easier, but still challenging, route, cross the rock-ribbed creekbed and continue on the left side of the drainage.

At mile 3.2, the trail climbs to meet stands of aspen and passes a colony of **false hellebore** that hangs out in a creekcrossing with **brown-eyed Susan.**

A zigzag of switchbacks leads to a final slog up the rocky slope of the canyon that finally ends at FR 300. Return the way you came.

Wildflower Hike 21

Horton Creek Trail

A trio of Parry's agave in the shaded forest of the Horton Creek Trail.

Trail Rating	Moderate
Trail Length	3 miles one way
Location	Payson
Elevation	5,400–6,650 feet
Contact	Tonto National Forest, Payson Ranger District, 928-474-7900
Bloom Season	July–September
Peak Bloom	August
Directions	From Payson, drive 15.8 miles east on AZ 260 and turn left (north) onto FR 289. Drive 0.8 mile to the trailhead parking area on the left side of the road, across from the Upper Tonto Creek Campground. Cross the road and enter the campground to get to the trail.

Horton Creek is named for homesteader Willis B. Horton, who lived along the creek in the late 1800s. It starts as Horton Springs, gushing from the side of Arizona's backbone, the Mogollon Rim. The trail follows the creek up to its start at the base of the Mogollon Rim.

Look for flowers as soon as you cross the road from the parking area to the trailhead. **Canyon grape** drapes across bushes and grasses. If you look closely, you can see small clusters of flowers in early summer and grapes by August, dripping from its tendriled vine. **Mullein** stretches its columnar stem above tall grasses. **Hooker's evening primrose** lines up along the roadsides.

Once on the path, **Mexican woollywhite, scarlet gaura,** and **wild geranium** spread under a manmade rock wall that slopes up to the Upper Tonto Creek Campground. **Meadow rue** and **wild geranium** cluster around a trailhead sign.

The trail immediately drops into the Horton Creek drainage and spends only a moment there before it climbs out. While in the drainage, observe **Hooker's evening primrose** in all its bloom stages: podlike buds to beautiful large yellow flowers to the orange tint on its wilted blossoms. **Arizona rose** bushes blush with red hips. The drainage widens and passes a colony of **dogbane** just before the trail heads out of it.

Graham's tick clover and **white snakeroot** brush against the trail on its rocky climb out of the drainage; the trail then follows the drainage on an old jeep road with these wildflowers in tow. The rocky north slope invites **sweet scent** and **scruffy prairie clover.** Watch, too, for **antelope horns.** This attractive milkweed gets its name from its curved seedpods that split into "horns."

Black medick, short for the clover's scientific name, *Medicago*, lines the trail. Its

WOODLAND PINEDROPS
Pterospora andromedea

Most everything about woodland pinedrops—from their ivory urn-shaped flowers to their sticky red stem—is unusual. The name comes from the Greek words *pteron,* meaning "wing," and *sporos,* meaning "seed," referring to the netlike wing on one end of its tiny seeds.

Woodland pinedrops are not typical plants because they don't have a trace of chlorophyll. This feature might indicate a parasite, but woodland pinedrops don't belong in that category. Rather, they are classified as saprophytes.

Parasites, such as mistletoe and dodder, thrive on living material such as oak trees and plants. Saprophytes, however, live on decaying organic materials in the soil. You can find woodland pinedrops in the rich soil of coniferous forests.

small yellow pea flower grows from dark-green clover leaves. **Canyon grape** and **Virginia creeper**, both members of the grape family that bloom inconspicuous greenish flowers in the spring, take advantage of the moist environment, draping down and coiling around trees.

Golden-beard penstemon and **Indian paintbrush** color a clearing right before an S-gate. Just after the gate, **bergamot** forms colonies between **wild chrysanthemum**, **spreading four o'clock**, and **New Mexico yellow flax**. A bit farther, **large-flowered brickellbush** will gather around dainty **scarlet gaura**. **Goldenrod** and **little leaf globemallow** contribute bright gold and orange outbursts of color.

In a meadow at about mile 0.5, watch how **cleavers** crawl in a jumble of boulders along the trail. Also watch for **many-flowered gromwell** along the path. Pine trees are momentary interlopers in the meadow, but their shade filters the heat of the sun enough to draw **red cinquefoil, silver-stem lupine,** and **yarrow**. Another meadow has **butterfly weed** beaming through hip-high grass. This wildflower exhibits its connection to the milkweed family by the upright pods it displays after its cluster of orange flowers has bloomed. The flat-topped clusters make a perfect landing pad for butterflies.

Silver-stem lupine fills a clearing on the west side of the trail, and **Fendler's ceanothus** lines the other side. **Mexican woollywhite, goldenrod,** and **Wright's deervetch** drop gold onto the trailsides, mixing with pale purple **many-flowered gilia** and **narrow-leaf penstemon**.

At about mile 0.75, the trail enters a brushy section lined with **point leaf manzanita** and **Fendler's ceanothus**. The path passes a colony of **bracken fern** at mile 1, but take a moment to look into the forest on the east side of the trail. A trio of **Parry's agave** makes a curious appearance. Usually found on dry, rocky, and sun-drenched slopes, the agave makes an ill fit on the fern-covered forest floor. More appropriately, **Fendler's hawkweed** mixes its velvet leaves in with the ferns.

Continuing in the bushes, and now on a rock-ribbed section of road, the trail climbs with the sound of the creek always nearby. **Arizona thistle** displays distinctive rose-colored flower heads much more slender than typical thistles. **Sweet scent** appears in clusters along the trail's edge. Its small lavender flowers might, at a quick glance, be confused with **many-flowered gilia**. But the flowers belong to two different families, and have completely different shapes.

Erosion has carved several narrow channels leading into the trail that eventually drain into Horton Creek. Look for **nodding onion** at these drainages. This lily family member likes the extra moisture the drainages provide.

Just past a deep gully filled with the purple from **wild geranium**, the trail takes a short downhill stretch where **New Mexico yellow flax** appears. When the trail levels out, **agrimonia** and **many-flowered gromwell** come

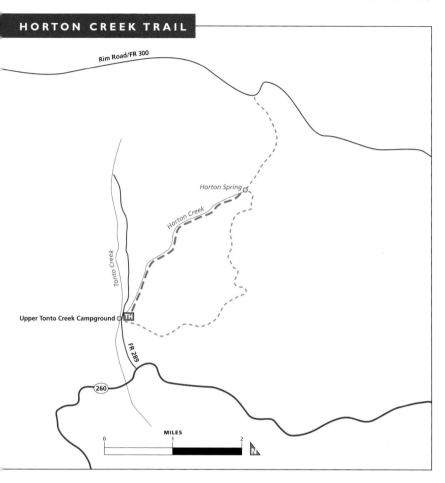

HORTON CREEK TRAIL

Rim Road/FR 300

Horton Spring

Horton Creek

Tonto Creek

Upper Tonto Creek Campground   TH

FR 289

260

MILES

0   1   2

N

trailside. This moist section appeals to **heal all** and **yellow columbine**, as well as **poison ivy**.

The trail edges the creek several feet below, then quickly meets it again at mile 2 where the creek cascades over a ledge of red sandstone. Take a moment and drop into the drainage where **agrimonia** crowds the banks and **yellow columbine** nod their bonnetlike flowers over the crystal water.

Mats of **watercress** spread near the creekbanks. This mustard family member imparts a peppery taste. The tiny white flowers' scientific name, *Nasturtium officinale*, hints at this pungency in a poetic way. *Nasturtium* comes from the Latin, *nasi tortium*, meaning "distortion of the nose," referring to its sharpness.

Trout fishermen should look for mats of **watercress**. Besides harboring freshwater insects, trout's favorite food, the floating network of plants makes an excellent cover for the fish in Horton Creek.

While the trail continues close to the creek, look for forest lovers like **Canada violet** and **woodland pinedrops**. At a pile of boulders, the trail pulls away from the water and starts climbing up the Mogollon Rim along the edge of a mixed conifer forest, eventually ducking under its cover.

When you come to another fork in the trail, you have two choices. If you veer left, you have a dry slog on the trail up to Horton Springs. If you veer right, you will follow an unmaintained path that climbs a steep grade along the creek, looking down on cascades that splash over moss-covered rocks as it rushes down the mountain. Take the unmaintained path only if you have good route-finding skills.

At the spring, **yellow columbine** arches golden flower heads over the crystal waters. **Brown-eyed Susan** stands along the creekbanks with **false Solomon's seal** and **heal all**. **Watercress** forms islands of green speckled with white racemes of flowers in pools where trout splash. Return the way you came.

The Horton Creek Trail passes through clearings lush from the moisture of nearby Horton Creek.

Pine Canyon Trail

This trail goes down from the Mogollon Rim to a verdant forest along Pine Creek.

Because of its relatively quick descent into Pine Canyon, this trail passes a variety of different wildflowers. Its start along a drainage draws moisture-loving flowers, then its passage through a dry pine forest attracts flowers requiring less water. The downhill switchback even features high-desert flowers. The trail finally lands on the canyon floor, nurtured by Pine Creek, and into a wonderful collection of wildflowers.

An old ranch road starts the trail in a ponderosa pine forest. The pines let in enough sunlight to attract **silver-stem lupine**. After a short downhill coast to a drainage, the trail lands next to a colony of **thermopsis**. Also called golden pea due to its yellow pealike clusters, **thermopsis** blooms in the spring. Look for **red cinquefoil** and **wild geranium** nearby.

Trail Rating	Strenuous
Trail Length	3–8 miles one way
Location	The Mogollon Rim near Pine
Elevation	5,400–7,200 feet
Contact	Tonto National Forest, Payson Ranger District, 928-474-7900
Bloom Season	July–early September
Peak Bloom	August
Directions	From Pine, drive north on AZ 87 about 1.1 miles past its junction with AZ 260. Turn right (south) and proceed through the gate (be sure to close it) 0.1 mile to a parking area at the trailhead. To arrange a shuttle hike, leave a vehicle at the signed trailhead just south of the town of Pine.

Brambles of **red raspberry** thrive in the drainage, and **bracted strawberry** lines the edges of the road. **Red raspberry** brambles follow the road as it parallels the drainage. Watch, too, for **Nuttall's linanthus, mountain parsley,** and **Arizona cudweed.** When the trail comes to a fork at about mile 0.2, veer right to continue on the Pine Canyon Trail.

The trail climbs out of the drainage to a drier environment that supports **Wright's deervetch** and **wild chrysanthemum. Point leaf manzanita** bushes meet with **Fendler's ceanothus** along the roadsides. **Ceanothus** will have clusters of small white flowers blooming at its tips in August, but **point leaf manzanita** blooms earlier in May. You can still recognize **point leaf manzanita** by its smooth, mahogany-colored limbs. Spreads of **goldeneye, goldenrod,** and **Arizona cudweed** like to gather in pockets between the bushes.

At another fork, about mile 0.3, veer left. Purple-hued **many-flowered gilia** makes a bold color combination with **golden aster.** A few steps farther, **Mexican silene** adds red-orange to the mix.

As the trail drops toward the edge of the Mogollon Rim, the route makes a natural path for runoff during wet weather and attracts a strong showing of wildflowers. At the Rim, look for **scruffy prairie clover.**

The trail zigzags below the Rim down the south face of the Coconino sandstone canyon wall, picking through cobbles and hobbling down sandstone slabs while it shows off stunning views of the canyon system. Ledges of sandstone become rock gardens where **Indian paintbrush** and **golden-beard penstemon** add striking red colors to the buff sandstone's blush. **Antelope sage** and **fleabane** add fresh white flowers. **Pink windmill** and **verbena** color the sandstone with pink and purple flowers. High-desert vegetation of **Parry's agave, point leaf manzanita**, and scrub oak thrive in the sun-drenched environment.

The wildflowers thin as the trail digs into the canyon on this exposed section. Still, a colony of **New Mexico yellow flax** gathers at about mile 1 near a wooden sign announcing switchbacks, which is also surrounded by **western dayflower.**

At the intersection with the Spalding Canyon Trail, about mile 1.5, the trail ducks under pines and the wildflowers return. Moist crooks gather colonies of **poison ivy** and scatterings of **Nuttall's linanthus, western dayflower,** and **pink windmill.** At mile 1.75, the trail intersects with the Cinch Hook Trail. Both of these side canyon routes climb about 1.5 miles back up to AZ 87 on the Mogollon Rim.

As the trail reaches Pine Creek, around mile 2, the environment suddenly shifts. The creek's presence coaxes moisture-loving botanicals to show up. **Horsetail** congregates around the creek and **Canada violet** lines the shady sections of trail, appearing often in this wooded section of the trail.

The white flowers of the **Canada violet** have a pristine aspect and freshness that evoke the Elizabethan's connection of the violet with guileless love. On the other hand, the fairy Puck concocted a potion using violet juice in *A Midsummer Night's Dream* to make "man or woman madly dote / Upon the next live creature that it sees."

Violet flowers do not produce seeds. They self-pollinate through a process called cleistogamy. Undeveloped violet flowers that have no petals, scent, or nectar self-pollinate through small anthers that contain a few pollen grains and a dwarfed pistil.

INDIAN PAINTBRUSH
Castilleja sp.

Arizona's Indian paintbrush flowers come in many colors, ranging from yellow to coral to rich red. This is not surprising, since the state has over a dozen different species of *Castilleja*. The bracts of Indian paintbrush give the plant its attractive characteristic of a tattered brush dipped in paint. The flowers usually dwell out of sight in the colorful bracts.

Like some other members of the figwort family, Indian paintbrush has a semiparasitic nature and produces only a portion of the food it requires. The plant gets the rest of its nutrients by tapping its roots into another plant's root system.

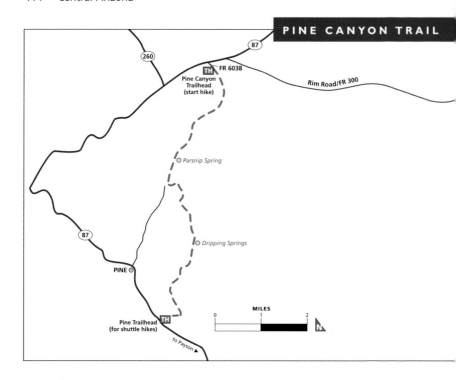

PINE CANYON TRAIL

These undeveloped flowers are always fertile, while the more perfect flowers are nearly, or completely, sterile.

White nightshade, Arizona rose, and **cleavers** appear in dapples of sunlight. Watch for **bergamot** when the trail cuts through a colony of **bracken fern**. When the trail basks in full sun, look for **large-flowered brickellbush** and **Thurber's stephanomeria.**

A rock-ribbed creekcrossing has **cinquefoil** and **agrimonia** lining up at the creekbanks. **Yellow columbine** and **Richardson's geranium** stay right in the drainage. A bit farther, **mountain lobelia** colonizes an area near a sign announcing a spur trail to Parsnip Spring, then lines the 50-foot-long path that takes you to the spring.

Back on the trail, watch for more **mountain lobelia** and **Hooker's evening primrose.** In a short distance, Parsnip Spring rambles across the trail as it makes its way to Pine Creek. The trail also heads toward the creek, nudging close enough to see **agrimonia** along its banks.

Just past the trail's junction with the Temple Canyon route, about mile 3, the trail climbs above the creek and provides views into it from a scenic vantage lined with **false Solomon's seal.** This makes a good turnaround point. From here, the trail pulls away from the creek and starts its 5-mile dry course to its end at the town of Pine. Return the way you came.

Canyon Creek

The Canyon Creek drainage grows so thickly with wildflowers that the beaten path often gets swallowed up by color.

Easy	***Trail Rating***
0.6 mile one way	***Trail Length***
Payson	***Location***
6,400 feet	***Elevation***
Tonto National Forest, Pleasant Valley Ranger District, 928-462-4300	***Contact***
July–September	***Bloom Season***
August	***Peak Bloom***
This hike has no maintained trail and requires rock-hopping. Wear footgear you don't mind getting wet. The OW Ranch, a working ranch upon the hill just east of the creek, is over 100 years old. Please respect all signs designating private property.	***Special Considerations***
From Payson, go east on AZ 260 31 miles and turn right (south) on FR 512 (Young Road). Drive 3 miles to FR 33 and turn left (east); go 2.9 miles to FR 34 and turn right (south). Go about 4.5 miles to the Canyon Creek bridge and park (where FR 34 meets FR 188, go straight on FR 188 which will then turn sharply to the north).	***Directions***

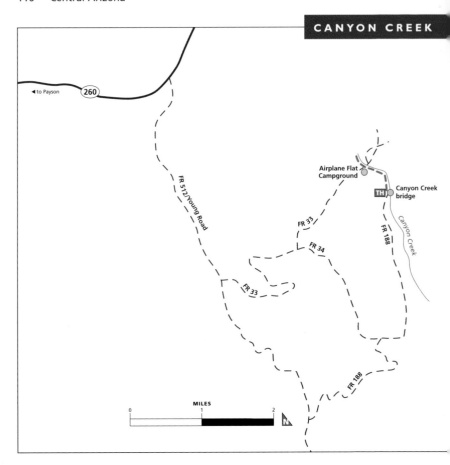

◄ to Payson   260

FR 512/Young Road

Airplane Flat
Campground

TH   Canyon Creek
bridge

FR 33

FR 34

FR 33

FR 188

Canyon Creek

FR 188

MILES
0   1   2
N

Canyon Creek, a blue-ribbon trout stream tucked away on the edge of the Tonto National Forest near the Fort Apache Indian Reservation, keeps a low enough profile that you may see more signs of animals than people. The cool canyon environment, forested canyon walls, and grassy meadows by the pristine creeksides provides an attractive and calming atmosphere.

When summer hits, the creek's banks overflow with wildflowers, turning the creek into a smorgasbord for wildlife. Animal tracks appear often along the creek. With that in mind, purify any creek water before you drink it.

Colonies of **goldenweed** lend a golden glow to the meadowed landscape around the parking area next to the creek. **Yarrow** and **Arizona cudweed** add white streaks in the golden glaze. A rocky mound on the west side of the parking area has a melange of **Arizona rose, tansy mustard, wild geranium,** and **western dayflower.**

Look for a faint path on the eastern side of the parking area to lead you to a gate that positions you next to the creek. The path brushes past **chicory** and yarrow. Blue **chicory** flowers open with the sun and last only a day. Their ground and roasted roots make the coffee additive so popular in the Cajun culture.

Once inside the fenceline on the creek's banks, spend some time identifying the wildflowers. Purple **wild geranium** and **spreading four o'clock** dot the meadow area, and mounds of **locoweed** paint the banks solid purple. **Mexican hat** adds rusty-red in the meadow with its velvet petals surrounding a raised cone. **Horehound** hugs a rocky patch.

Virgin's bower vine twists around a willow surrounded by **bergamot, Richardson's geranium,** and **larkspur. Virgin's bower** has no petals, but its four white sepals and numerous white stamens look like a ball of petals.

Creekwater braids around clumps of grass and **brown-eyed Susan.** Slender **willow weed** has tiny pink flowers. **Watercress** forms mats with white flowers in the water. The uncommon **New Mexico checkermallow** likes to practically stand in the creek, but you may find it several yards away from the stream in boggy areas.

As you head upstream on the route of least resistance (usually game trails), you may find elk tracks sunken into the soft earth or see a giant blue heron gliding silently overhead. A variety of songbirds will chatter and tweet in the surrounding trees. **Hop vine** hangs in willow limbs, **plains beebalm** and **scarlet gaura** like sunny spots, and **heal all** gathers next to the stream. **Mullein** likes to cozy next to willow snags and deadfall. **Mountain lobelia** and **red cinquefoil** tend to keep a short distance from the creek.

Near mile 0.3, beaver dams stretch across the creek and **brown-eyed Susan** borders the ponds. **Smartweed,** a member of the buckwheat family, raises pink clusters of flowers from shiny and leathery dark-green leaves at the ponds' edges.

Mountain lobelia brings a blue hue to the bench just north of the creek as it

VIRGIN'S BOWER
Clematis ligusticifolia

The white blossoms on the virgin's bower vine drape over trees and bushes, practically covering them at times. This *clematis* looks much different from its cousins. *Clematis* usually has four petals, but virgin's bower has four sepals and a burst of stamens that emit a fragrant smell. Virgin's bower produces a seed with a feathery tail.

Early settlers used an infusion of the peppery-tasting leaves and stems to relieve sore throats.

bends west between the beaver dams. **Hop vine** and **woolly morning glory** crawl across an old rock corral on the bench. The corral, which looks like a long pile of rocks, was probably used to hold cattle. Also watch for **plains beebalm** near the corral.

As you near the Airplane Flat Campground, about mile 0.4, look for a footpath on the east side of the creek. The path squeezes between **Arizona rose, agrimonia,** and **currant** bushes in a forest environment with **Richardson's geranium** and **Canada violet** spreading underneath.

The path exits the forest and passes through a meadow full of **fleabane** and **Arizona cudweed**. Watch for patches of **field mint**. This pink-flowered mint often exudes a strong mint scent when you crush its leaves or step on it. Close to the campground, look for a weak path that forks to the left to see a colony of **larkspur.**

When you reach the campground area, you may continue upstream in Canyon Creek, or return the way you came.

Sand Tank Canyon

*This backroad
route features
colorful high-
desert plants
and great views.*

I n the depths of summer, the high desert landscape along FR 433 displays
flowering stalks zooming upward from succulents, drought-tolerant
bushes displaying beautiful blossoms, colorful spreads of wildflowers along
the roadsides, and uncommon appearances by individual plants. Many
flowers are night bloomers, making the best time to take this hike early
morning or late afternoon.

The road passes through the Sierra Ancha Experimental Forest
where the Forest Service does research. The Forest Service did extensive
watershed research from post–World War II until the early 1970s, meas-
uring the amount and quality of water that flowed through the drainage.

Trail Rating	Moderate
Trail Length	2.7 miles one way
Location	Globe
Elevation	4,400–4,800 feet
Contact	Tonto National Forest, Pleasant Valley Ranger District, 928-462-4300
Bloom Season	March–September
Peak Bloom	Late March and August
Directions	From the intersection of US 60 and AZ 88 just west of Globe, drive 13.6 miles north on AZ 88 and turn right (north) onto AZ 288. Drive 18.1 miles to FR 488 and turn left (west); drive 0.1 mile and park at the bridge.

Remnants from the research, such as buildings and equipment, remain in the drainages along the road.

Judging by the animal prints you may see along the road (such as bobcat, deer, elk, bear, and mountain lion), the road is used more by wildlife than humans. Nevertheless, the route is considered multi-use, and hikers should be careful of motorized vehicles.

The route starts in a riparian area in the Parker Creek drainage. **Goldenrod** and **desert marigold** follow the route's descent into Sand Tank Canyon. **Desert marigold**, a popular spring flower, blooms year-round if it gets enough water.

Arizona sycamore trees stretch their silver-white limbs into the roadway past the juniper and oak trees lined along the roadsides. **Canyon grape** drapes over bushes and tree limbs. **Virgin's bower** twines its petalless white blooms in scrub oak bushes. The vine, once chewed by Indians and pioneers to relieve sore throats, has a peppery taste. A look into the drainage at about mile 0.2 might reveal cattails stuffed in the creekbed.

Sumac bushes present clusters of velvet red berries along the bottom of a large rock wall on the west side of the road. Right across the road from them, on the drainage side, **sacred datura** spreads under a thicket of **poison ivy** mingling with **red raspberry** brambles. Look for **red-dome blanketflower** along the road's edge, too.

A line of **skyrocket** leads to **lilac chaste tree** just before the road bends up and out of the drainage, at mile 0.4. An oriental native from China and India that escaped from cultivation into the wilds, the **lilac chaste tree** has palmate leaves akin to lupine. Its lavender cluster of five-lobed tubular flowers produce spicy berries. The tree's berries and spice-scented leaves explain its alternate names of Indian spice and monk's pepper tree.

The road separates from the riparian area and winds westward with **yerba santa** lined along its south side. Also called mountain balm, **yerba santa** has fragrant leaves—thin, sticky, and leathery—which have the medicinal property of soothing respiratory ailments.

After rising and falling over gentle terrain with scatterings of **desert marigold, verbena, many-flowered gilia,** and **western dayflower**, the road bends into the crook of a wash at about mile 0.8. Look for **snapdragon vine** in scrub oak on the north side of the road at the edge of the wash. A close look at the **snapdragon vine** shows its rose-colored snapdragon flowers have pink lines painted on its protruding ivory throat. The throat has a cover of fine hairs. The lines direct pollinators into the flower.

On the other side of the wash, a crumbling ledged rock wall has **sweet scent, Emory's comet milkweed,** and **spiny cliff-brake fern. Desert blazing star** bushes edge the inner bend of the road. Hooked hairs on the bush's gray-green leaves have a velcro feel and character. Called "tenacious" by the Navajos, the leaves stick to fabrics. The bright yellow flowers often open in the late afternoon.

You may see sticky **devil's claw** in the wash. This odd-shaped flower waits to bloom until the weather gets hot, then produces an extravagant fruit about a foot long that eventually splits open

DEVIL'S CLAW
Proboscidea parviflora

The light pink devil's claw prefers the desert regions of Arizona, appearing in disturbed areas such as roadsides, mesas, or washes. In the high desert, the hairy and sticky plant usually waits until summer to bloom.

The plant's name refers to the plant's foot-long curved fruit pod. The sticky pod bursts open at maturity to expose the woody skeleton that ends in two curved claws.

The Tohono O'odham used the fiber from devil's claw's pods for basketmaking materials. The longest pods produced the best fibers, and the Indians domesticated the plant to produce pods twice as long as wild varieties.

As menacing as the name devil's claw sounds, the plant actually has healing qualities. The plant has anti-inflammatory properties, and it lowers uric acid levels in the body. Both of these characteristics may have a soothing effect on gout and arthritis.

and sheds its skin, leaving a two-pronged woody skeleton. The skeleton gives the plant its name.

A bit farther down the road, **gum weed** splays sticky stems across a rusty bedrock surface along the road. A yellow daisy flower, also sticky, tops each stem. The whole plant exudes a resinous aroma.

At about mile 0.9, a drainage on the north side of the road has a concrete weir across it and a small shed—remnants from the area's water research days. You can see more paraphernalia at mile 1.1 in Parker Creek Canyon. Watch for an old wooden building in a side canyon above a culvert on the south wall of Parker Creek Canyon. This was a water measurement station, and the building housed the equipment.

At mile 1.2, the mouth of Parker Creek Canyon creates a fabulous panorama to the southwest. **Sotol** and **golden-flowered agave** jut from succulent basal leaves dotted on the landscape sloping into the canyon. The north side of the road has **sunbright** mixing with grasses. This portulaca family member has long succulent leaves that gather like a clump of grass at its base. A pretty pink star flower tops an 8-inch stem. An odd version of *Penstemon linarioides* shows up here, too. This variety, called **bushy linarioides**, has small purple flowers and is bushy rather than prostrate.

The road rises steeply, the jagged depths of Parker Creek Canyon appearing as you climb. **Fleabane** and **wild chrysanthemum** add white and yellow color along the road as it winds uphill, and white clusters of **wild buckwheat** and **yellow menodora** accent the coloration. Also watch for **wild four o'clock** arbitrarily appearing by the road. Its lovely lobed, pink, tube flowers are night bloomers, opening in late afternoon. **White ball acacia** dangles small white ball-shaped blossoms that develop into flat, brown seedpods.

WILD FOUR O'CLOCK
Mirabilis multiflora

The four o'clock family gets its name from its flowers' predisposition to open in the late afternoon and wither in the morning. If these night bloomers have a fragrance, it usually develops a couple hours after the flower opens.

The deep pink wild four o'clock flowers generate a musky odor. Once the odor kicks in, it starts attracting hawkmoths within minutes. Look for these pretty funnel flowers on rocky slopes or roadsides in high desert terrain.

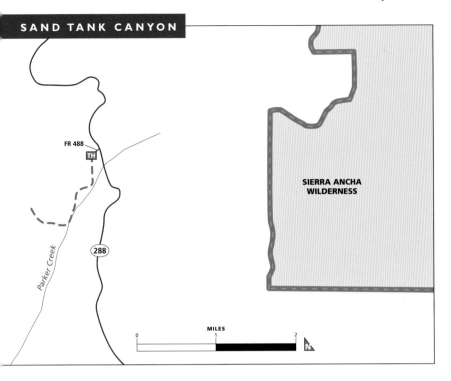

SAND TANK CANYON

FR 488

TH

Parker Creek

288

SIERRA ANCHA
WILDERNESS

MILES
0   1   2

Yellow menodora and Wright beeflower fill a field when the road tops out at mile 1.5. **Many-flowered gilia, bushy linarioides,** and **narrow-leaf penstemon** edge the road with shades of purple and a field of **wild buckwheat** surrounds **cane cholla** cactus.

At mile 1.8, the road gets brushy. Scrub oak and **point leaf manzanita** form a hedge along the road with pockets of color filled by **narrow-leaf penstemon, wild buckwheat,** and **yellow menodora.** Piñon and juniper trees rise in the background. Sometimes **skyrocket** and **Indian paintbrush** tangle in the brush.

The wildflowers strengthen again by about mile 2.5. Watch for beautiful light-orange **sida** of the mallow family edging the road. The purple and yellow blossom of **tansyleaf spine aster** leads to a colony of **silverleaf nightshade** just before the road's end.

A view point at the road's end gives you a 360-degree panorama: Parker Creek Canyon in the south, Roosevelt Lake backdropped by the Four Peaks to the west, the Salome Wilderness in the north, and the Sierra Ancha Mountains in the east. Return the way you came.

Parker Creek Canyon Overlook

Hikers encounter a variety of high-desert plants on this hike.

The high-desert terrain over which FR 140 passes draws a number of plants to its piñon-juniper landscape. The more noticeable—and more expected—agaves, sotol, and banana yucca gather in this exposed high desert, but more unusual plants gather along the roadside as well.

The route starts at an overlook of Parker Creek Canyon. The view shows the jagged features of Parker Creek Canyon and a dramatic panorama of Roosevelt Lake with the Four Peaks rising behind.

Trail Rating	Easy
Trail Length	0.7 mile one way
Location	Globe
Elevation	4,500–4,600 feet
Contact	Tonto National Forest, Pleasant Valley Ranger District, 928-462-4300
Bloom Season	March–September
Peak Bloom	August
Directions	From the intersection of US 60 and AZ 88 just west of Globe, drive 13.6 miles north on AZ 88 and turn right (north) onto AZ 288; drive 16.2 miles to FR 140 and turn left (west); drive 0.7 mile to the parking area.

PARKER CREEK CANYON OVERLOOK

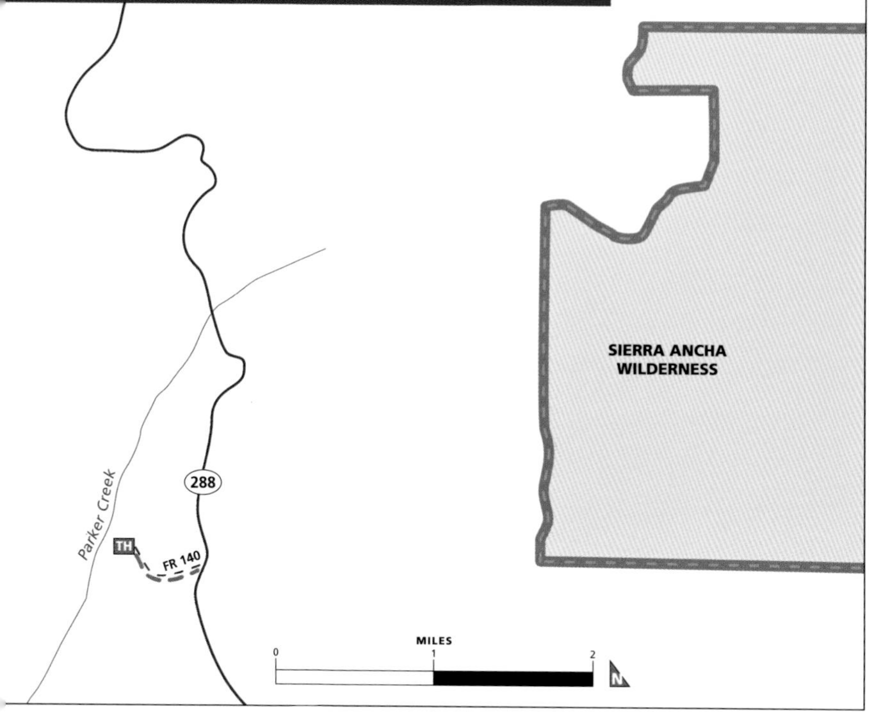

SIERRA ANCHA
WILDERNESS

Parker Creek

288

TH

FR 140

MILES

0   1   2

N

After you enjoy the panorama, take a look around the grassy field in front of the canyon rim. **Tansyleaf spine aster** shows purple rays around gold disks. **Little leaf globemallow**, full of orange flowers, borders the road. Two members of the portulaca family, **sunbright** and **purslane**, show off beautiful blossoms. **Sunbright** has light-pink star flowers and **purslane** has copper-colored petals with magenta-tinged bases. **Purslane**, especially, prefers to dwell around the rim of the canyon.

Backtracking along the road, watch for **desert senna** and poisonous **whorled milkweed** when the road curves eastward. Like most milkweeds, **whorled milkweed** has hoods rising from a pedestal in each flower. The slits between the hoods trap a pollinator's leg. As the insect pulls its leg free, pollen attaches to the leg, ready to pollinate the next flower the pollinator stops at during the same leg-hold process.

Sunflower rises above meadow grasses that spread from the road. **Fleabane** and **wild buckwheat** give a silver-white sheen to the meadow.

At mile 0.25, **yellow menodora, wild buckwheat,** and **narrow-leaf penstemon** circulate their colors in pockets between the high-desert vegetation of scrub oak, **banana yucca,** and piñon pine. **Wild chrysanthemum** stays along the road's edges with **tansyleaf spine aster.**

Desert marigold and **bushy linarioides** (an unusual variety of penstemon with small purple flowers) meet in a shallow drainage at a low point in the road at mile 0.4.

When the road starts to climb out of the drainage, it

DESERT BLAZING STAR
Mentzelia pumila

The desert blazing star bush doesn't grow very large, as its scientific name (*pumila,* meaning *small* or *dwarf*) suggests; it may grow up to 2 feet. The leaves have an unobtrusive gray-green color and the bushes appear sparingly in the high desert.

The flowers are, as its common name implies, the star of the show. Pretty, bright yellow, and star shaped, the flowers often open in the late afternoon from April through early September.

The leaves of the bush provoked the Navajo to call the plant "tenacious." Hooked hairs on the leaves cause them to cling to fabric.

enters a brushy corridor of scrub oak, **skunkbush**, and **point leaf manzanita.** Skunkbush's yellow clusters of flowers bloom in early spring, and the pinkish bell flowers of the **point leaf manzanita** in April or May.

Little mounds of **rattlesnake weed** clump on the road as it climbs the hill. This spurge family plant has tiny white flowers with a maroon mark at their centers. Its milky sap gives the plant a sticky feel. The sap may cause irritation in some people, but was once considered a potent remedy for snake bites.

Watch for a line of **desert blazing star** bushes at about mile 0.6. The bush's showy flowers bloom bright yellow. Its seedpod rattles when shaken. The best time to view **desert blazing star** is late afternoon when the flowers open.

You may spot two different parasitic plants along the road. One, **mistletoe**, lives in the scrub oak bushes. Over time, this parasite plant can kill its host by depleting it of moisture and nutrients.

The other parasitic plant you may see is **dodder**. Looking like a golden thread strangling its host plant, **dodder** blooms tiny cream clusters of flowers in the summer. You may see **dodder** wringing around bushes along the road, specifically **yerba santa. Yerba santa** has thin, shiny, dark leaves and blooms pale lavender funnel flowers with five lobes.

As the trail nears the road, **verbena** paints streaks of purple in spreads of **yellow menodora. Narrow-leaf pentstemon** forms pools of purple that flow in pockets of brush. Just about at road's end, look for more **desert blazing star,** big white trumpet flowers on **sacred datura,** and **clammyweed.**

PURSLANE
Portulaca suffrutescens

The purslane flower's beautiful blend of color makes it a pleasing find. Its five coppery-orange petals have tinges of magenta on their bases. A magenta stigma has a crowd of anthers around it. If you viewed purslane under a microscope, you would see that the flower's beauty goes beyond skin deep.

On the surface, you would never know the fertilized purslane produces a fascinating cache of seeds just as attractive as its blossom. Seed containers that look like miniature acorns burst open to expose seeds the size of a pinhead. The seeds have black and white markings pretty enough to string into a necklace if they were beads.

Wildflower Hike 26 Bear Wallow Trail

Trailsides are packed with wildflowers on the Bear Wallow Trail.

Bear wallows were a common occurrence in this drainage when rancher Pete Slaughter drove cattle through it in the late 1800s. Bears liked to laze in the wallows in the summertime to relieve themselves of biting flies. They still like to hang out in Bear Wallow Canyon. Catching a glimpse of one (or an elk, mountain lion, or even a Mexican gray wolf) or at least seeing signs of its presence is not unusual.

The remote drainage, with its perennial water source, makes an attractive habitat for these animals. It also provides excellent conditions for wildflowers. You may see several dozen wildflower species on your hike.

Trail Rating	Moderate
Trail Length	2.6–7.5 miles one way
Location	Bear Wallow Wilderness
Elevation	6,800–8,400 feet
Contact	Apache-Sitgreaves National Forest, Alpine Ranger District, 928-339-4384
Bloom Season	July–September
Peak Bloom	August
Special Considerations	This trail is located in the Bear Wallow Wilderness where no mechanized vehicles, including mountain bikes, are allowed.
Directions	From Alpine, drive south on US 191 about 22 miles to Hannagan Meadow. Drive another 5 miles south on US 191 and turn right (west) onto FR 25. Drive about 3 miles to the signed trailhead on the left.

The trail starts on a 1.5-mile path that leads to the North Fork of Bear Wallow Creek. The trail then parallels the North Fork, meeting up with Bear Wallow Creek, and follows the creek to just shy of the creek's confluence with the Black River on the San Carlos Indian Reservation. Along the way, the Reno and Gobbler Point trails intersect with the Bear Wallow Trail and provide access back to FR 25 for loop hikes.

After the trail crosses an unmarked road (look for cairns if there is no sign indicating where the trail picks up on the other side of the road), the path enters a mixed conifer forest laced with meadows. **Spur gentian** and **mountain parsley** lay streaks of yellow along the path. **Aspen fleabane, silver-stem lupine,** and **harebell** add purple hues. Don't overlook **Whipple's penstemon**, almost the same color as the lupine.

Sneezeweed gathers in the soggy lowlands of the field. Tiger moths, with black and white geometric-lined wings, like to park on the large daisy flowers.

Mixed conifers weave across the meadows like a dark matrix, compelling sun-loving flowers into clusters. **Osha** edges the fields, keeping to the lowpoints near the **sneezeweed**, then approaches the trail as the path starts to drop toward the Bear Wallow drainage. **Scouler's catchfly** sporadically lines the path. The unusual mauve flower keeps a distinctive appearance even when it has wilted to a striped calyx.

The trail, steep and rocky, doubles as a drainage in wet weather. Pools form along the path, keeping **osha** nearby. The tall pink flowers around the pools are **New Mexico checkermallow.** You always see checkermallow, not a common flower, near water.

After you have passed through and latched a gate at about mile 0.6, watch for tall **monkshood** to gather in the drainage with **towering polemonium. Red cinquefoil, Canada violet, thimbleberry,** and **verileaf phacelia** prefer to line the path. As the trail approaches the Bear Wallow drainage, **Arizona rose** encroaches into the path.

At mile 1.5, the trail reaches the North Fork of Bear Wallow Creek. Many of the wildflowers that appeared on the way down to the drainage follow the trail as it parallels the creek. The meadows between stands of aspen and mixed conifers attract **harebell, Indian paintbrush,** and **cinquefoil. Bergamot** fills pockets of sun in the trees. A jagged section of bedrock on the north side of the trail provides a dry venue for **spreading four o'clock, wild geranium, plains beebalm, golden-beard penstemon,** and **skyrocket.**

A couple of boggy meetings with the creek will put you in the middle of a gathering of **red cinquefoil, brown-eyed Susan,** and **osha.** Watch for colonies of **heal all** in these areas, too. During creekside sections, look for **Franciscan bluebell, St. John's wort,** and **curly dock** on the banks.

The trail squeezes through a corridor stuffed with lush vegetation. The long stems of **red figwort,** with its tiny red-tinged flowers, bend into the path lined with **nightshade** and

OSHA
Ligusticum porteri

The tall osha plant often appears in well-watered areas in the high country. Mountain streams with a good dose of sunlight almost always have a colony of osha displaying their white umbels along the water's edge.

As a member of the parsley family, osha resembles its cousin celery in appearance and scent. You can interchange the two in recipes. Herbalists use osha roots for pulmonary ailments. *A word of warning:* if you plan to ingest any part of the plant, make sure you don't confuse it with its highly poisonous hemlock cousins.

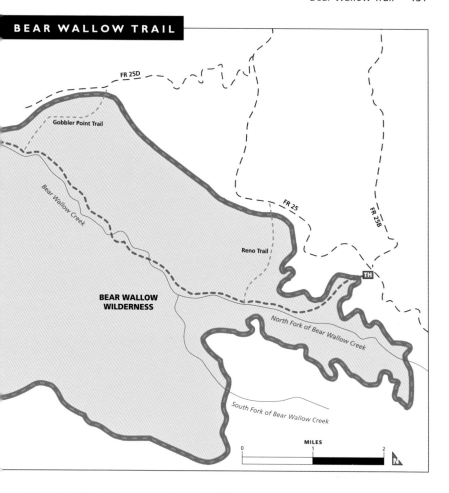

FR 25D

Gobbler Point Trail

Bear Wallow Creek

FR 25

Reno Trail

FR 25B

TH

**BEAR WALLOW
WILDERNESS**

North Fork of Bear Wallow Creek

South Fork of Bear Wallow Creek

MILES
0   1   2
N

poison ivy. Hop vine strings through foliage, ripe with its green fruit of over-lapping bracts.

At mile 1.6, the trail intersects with the Reno Trail, a good turnaround point for a day hike. But just beyond the intersection, the trail meets with Bear Wallow Creek. The area grows even more lush here, and it's worth hiking another mile or two to check it out.

Once you have decided your turnaround point, you may return the way you came, or make a loop by taking either the Reno or Gobbler Point Trail back to the rim and FR 25 back to your vehicle.

*Wildflower
Hike 27*

KP Creek Trail

*The KP Creek
Trail harbors
dozens of species
of wildflowers.*

This hike follows the South Fork of KP Creek as it tumbles 2.9 miles and 1,160 feet to its confluence with the North Fork of KP Creek. The two creeks combine at this point to form KP Creek. The trail continues another 6.5 miles, following KP Creek much of the way.

This hike follows only the South Fork of KP Creek. The path travels predominantly through a wooded canyon of mixed conifers and aspen trees —prime spotted owl habitat. You may see one of the brown and white raptors flapping below the treetops, or you may hear its doglike barks and cries. You may also get a glimpse of a Mexican gray wolf.

Trail Rating	Moderate
Trail Length	2.9 miles one way
Location	Alpine
Elevation	7,800–8,960 feet
Contact	Apache-Sitgreaves National Forest, Alpine Ranger District, 928-339-4384
Bloom Season	June–September
Peak Bloom	August
Special Considerations	This trail is located in the Blue Range Primitive Area where no mechanized vehicles, including mountain bikes, are allowed.
Directions	From Alpine, drive south on US 191 about 28 miles to the signed turnoff to the KP Campground and turn left (east); drive 1.2 miles to the trailhead.

Even if you do not see any wildlife along the trail, you can count on seeing an outstanding show of wildflowers. Throughout this wild and remote environment, you may identify several dozen different wildflower species.

The trail gets its start in a sunny meadow called a cienega, a name for a wetland fed by groundwater. The patches of **Rocky Mountain iris** that dwell in the soggy lowlands of the meadow bloom in June. In the summer, colonies of **sneezeweed, mountain lobelia,** and **gentiana** color the grasses. **Princely daisy, evening primrose,** and **yarrow** braid their purple, yellow, and white flowers in with the purple meadow grasses.

Just before the trail enters the woods, about mile 0.1, it squishes through a stream stuffed with water-loving plants. **Cow clover** edges the stream with **curly dock** and **willow weed. Osha** and **brown-eyed Susan** stand with **New Mexico checkermallow** and **polemonium. Buttercup** and **field mint** spread from the stream's banks. A mossy outcropping on the left has **Cockerell's sedum, wood sorrel,** and **cinquefoil** climbing all over it.

Once you're in the forest's shade, the variety of wildflowers changes. **Yarrow** and **princely daisy** make a pretty combination on the east side of the trail, while **Scouler's catchfly** and **harebell** cling together on the west side. **Canada violet** crowds under the boughlines of spruce trees. Heading deeper into the forest on the downhill, the trail passes **false Solomon's seal**. Its white cluster of berries will turn dark blue by the end of the summer. **Sweet Cicely** and **polemonium** grow in the dapples of sunlight allowed on the forest floor. **Bracted strawberry** edges the trail with **mouse-ear chickweed** and **mountain parsley.**

A large colony of **thermopsis**, some still clinging to the seedpods their yellow flower clusters left behind from their June blooms, leads up to a clearing. The sunshine attracts **red cinquefoil** and **plains beebalm** to the trail. **Indian paintbrush** and **golden-beard penstemon** display eye-catching red flowers. Purple-colored **polemonium** mix with **silver-stem lupine.**

These flowers stick with the trail until it enters an aspen stand at about mile 0.6. Watch how the florals transition to forest dwellers, such as **thimbleberry, meadow rue,** and **cleavers. Verileaf phacelia** appears in shady crooks. **Red cinquefoil** and **Indian paintbrush** splash red where the sun peeks in.

As the trail continues its descent to the South Fork of KP Creek, **spur gentian** and **orange gooseberry** take to exposed, sunny hillsides, where you should also look for **plains beebalm, trailing four o'clock,** and **pink windmill.** A blend of **Richardson's geranium** and **red cinquefoil** makes a striking combination.

The trail follows two tight switchbacks and lands on the canyon bottom at mile 0.9. Once creekside, the trail enters yet another environment—a wet world where cascades flow, moss-covered rocks scatter on the canyonslopes, and tree trunks drip with lichen.

Right away, you notice bright-yellow **brown-eyed Susan** gathered by the creek. Pink **New Mexico checkermallow** edges up to the water. Stalks of **false hellebore** and **Franciscan bluebell** dwell around pools and **watercress** dives right in. The trail begins to parallel the creek, flowers in tow, adding **baneberry** and **yellow columbine**, as it continues towards KP Creek.

SHOOTING STAR
Dodecatheon sp.

Consider spotting a colony of shooting star as a special occasion. The flower, barely an inch long, has swept-back petals suggestive of its common name. It has a showy quality common to the primrose family.

Shooting star comes in different colors, from white to a blush of pink or a bold rose-purple, and prefers damp, shady spots or areas next to mountain streams.

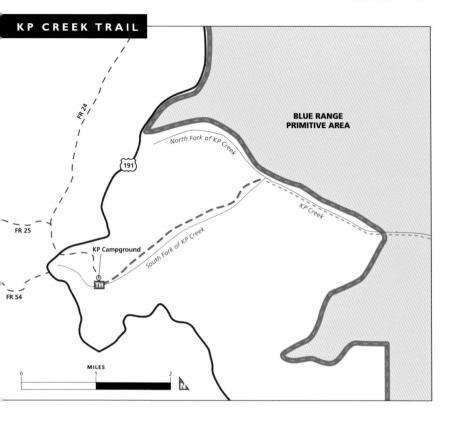

KP CREEK TRAIL

FR 24

BLUE RANGE
PRIMITIVE AREA

North Fork of KP Creek

191

KP Creek

FR 25

KP Campground

South Fork of KP Creek

FR 54

TH

MILES
0   1   2

Bigleaf avens and green pyrola also appear, but sparingly. Bigleaf avens, a member of the rose family, has yellow, waxy-looking flowers. Their leaves are bristly and toothed. The green pyrola has leafless stems rising from basal leaves that hang with small bell flowers. These wildflowers, though not in the same genus, go by the name of wintergreen.

Just after a creekcrossing, at about mile 1.3, watch for spur gentian on an upslope left of the trail. Sidestep a giant deadfall at about mile 1.7 by detouring to the left of it. Then check for fireweed on the edges of the creek.

When it enters an aspen stand, about mile 1.9, the creek gets brushy with New Mexico locust and red-osier dogwood. Neither early-blooming bush will have flowers in August, but the red-osier dogwood should have berries.

A large colony of polemonium comes to the trail just before a creek-crossing at mile 2. At the stream, agrimonia mixes with its cousin, Arizona rose. Bergamot, Hooker's evening primrose, and red cinquefoil crowd in the background, but poison ivy proliferates. The bergamot follows the trail as it leaves the drainage, creating purple spreads on the canyonslope.

At about mile 2.5 the trees tighten around the creek and cocoon it in more shade. Moss covers the rocks along the path, and forest-loving botanicals fill the trailsides. **Bracted strawberry, death camas,** and **thimbleberry** grow thick in this forest environment. Near a creekcrossing, look for **pinesap.** The red saprophytic flower looks like a fungus.

The next creekcrossing, mile 2.7, brushes up to a rock wall. White **shooting star** makes a rare appearance, covering the wall alongside the more common **wood sorrel** and cascades of **large-flowered brickellbush. Monkshood** waits on the other side of the creek.

The trail climbs out of the South Fork drainage and crosses a slope where **skyrocket** and **red cinquefoil** bask in the sun, then bends to the west where **mountain parsley** speckles the sun-dappled ground. After a few switchbacks bring the trail back into the drainage, rather than crossing the creek to continue on the KP Trail, take a hairpin right and follow a path down to a waterfall and the confluence of the north and south forks where they form KP Creek. At the confluence, look for **slender bog orchid** along the banks of the creek. Return the way you came.

Upper Fish Creek Trail

*Upper Fish Creek Trail passes through a variety of landscapes,
from a dark, damp aspen-fir forest to a sundrenched meadow.*

Moderate	*Trail Rating*
1.5 miles one way	*Trail Length*
Hannagan Meadow	*Location*
8,500–9,120 feet	*Elevation*
Apache-Sitgreaves National Forest, Alpine Ranger District, 928-339-4384	*Contact*
July–September	*Bloom Season*
August	*Peak Bloom*
From Hannagan Meadow, drive south 0.25 mile on US 191 to the signed trailhead on the right (west) side of the road.	*Directions*

This hike follows a section of the Fish Creek Trail, which travels on an old road that took ranchers and loggers down to Fish Creek. This section of trail, with its easy access, short length, and unique assortment of wildflowers, makes an excellent wildflower hike.

The trail starts in a tight-knit aspen forest where wildflowers wear pale colors. **Richardson's geranium** and **Canada violet** like the cloistering shade. A clearing at about mile 0.2 fills with sunny colors of **sneezeweed** and **Indian paintbrush**, along with moody purple-blue tones of **harebell** and **silver-stem lupine**. The path winds around in a switchback and passes through two more meadows with the same flowers. Then the trail dives steeply into a fir-aspen forest.

Heading downhill, the trail passes an extraordinary area rich in forest wildflowers. Stop a moment and take a close look along the trailsides 50 feet in any direction, and you can find over two dozen different flowers. The trail makes a sharp right turn at about mile 0.5.

You may notice the bell flowers of the very poisonous **death camas** growing near the bend. Then look for **green pyrola** and **side-bell pyrola**. These two members of the pyrola family have bell flowers growing on one or both sides of their leafless stems.

A light-green orchid, the tiny-flowered **slender bog orchid** grows trailside. Watch for another orchid species, **giant rattlesnake plantain,** with its tiny white flowers growing from a basal rosette of leaves marked with a mottled white line. You may also find **dwarf rattlesnake plantain**. Like its cousin **giant rattlesnake plantain**, the dwarf plantain has tiny white flowers, but only on one side of the leafless stem, rather than both.

Upslope, **spur gentian** have pale-yellow flowers. **Sweet Cicely's** tiny white flowers are barely noticeable. The leaves, however, emit a strong anise smell when crushed.

Baneberry's red berries and the reddish stems of **woodland pinedrops** add color also.

DEATH CAMAS
Zigadenus virescens

The greenish-white flowers of the death camas hang like bells down a 1- or 2-foot-long stem. An unusual find that prefers coniferous forests with rich soil, death camas' flowers bloom all summer long. Its cousin, elegant camas, also has an elongated cluster of white flowers, but faces upright to show a green heart-shaped gland at its base.

Both of these lily family members can be fatal if ingested. A heart depressant, zygadenine, resides in every part of the plants, from their charming flowers to their onion-shaped roots.

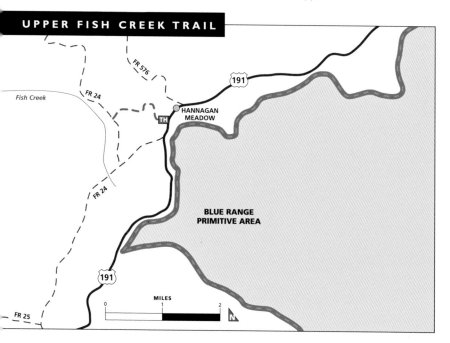

UPPER FISH CREEK TRAIL

Farther along on the trail, **sneezeweed** takes advantage of sunny slivers along the path, a signal the forest is thinning as it approaches a broad meadow. **Bracken fern** and **thermopsis** mingle on the forest floor, and follow the trail to the meadow at about mile 0.75.

The trail stays on the outer perimeter of the meadow as it continues near the edge of the forest. The path gives you a pretty panoramic view of the dipping meadow and the wildflowers that inhabit it. Orange-gold **sneezeweed** variegates a spread of **harebell. False hellebore** lines up in the meadow's lowland and mingles with **brown-eyed Susan**, attracted by the lowland's flow of water.

At about mile 1, a sign nailed to a ponderosa pine tree directs you to turn left for Fish Creek. The trail jumps a drainage full of **New Mexico checkermallow**, then follows more signs pointing to Fish Creek. Watch for colonies of **porch penstemon** along this portion of the trail.

The trail turns and enters a mixed conifer forest. **Mullein, golden aster,** and **fleabane** fill the upslope, and **red cinquefoil** edges the path. **Golden-beard penstemon** lines the rim of the downslope. The trail steps into the sunshine as it nears the end of this hike at FR 24. **Plains beebalm, pink windmill,** and **spreading four o'clock** like the sunny slope the trail passes. **New Mexico checkermallow** runs down a drainage on the slope to the road. **Yarrow** and **princely daisy** spread across the trail as it overlooks Fish Creek. You may continue on the Fish Creek Trail, located about 200 yards down FR 24, or you may return the way you came.

*Wildflower
Hike 29* *Lower Fish Creek Trail*

*This diverse
trail follows a
historic path to
the Black River.*

Fish Creek, named for its good fishing, travels through a particularly remote part of the White Mountains. Cradled in a cozy wooded canyon that opens up several times to accommodate meadows of wildflowers, the path follows a historical route used by cattlemen and forest rangers between Hannagan Meadow and the Black River.

The creek maintains a pure population of Arizona's state fish, the Apache trout, because of a barrier installed by the Arizona Game and Fish Department and the U.S. Forest Service across the creek. This barrier keeps the Black River's rainbow trout from hybridizing with the threatened natives.

Trail Rating	Moderate
Trail Length	5.5 miles one way
Location	Hannagan Meadow
Elevation	6,800–8,400 feet
Contact	Apache-Sitgreaves National Forest, Alpine Ranger District, 928-339-4384
Bloom Season	July–September
Peak Bloom	August
Special Considerations	High-clearance vehicles are necessary.
Directions	From Hannagan Meadow, drive 0.1 mile northeast on US 191 to FR 576 and turn left (west); drive about 4 miles to FR 24 and turn right (north); drive about 1 mile and turn left (west) on FR 83; drive about 4 miles and turn left (west) onto FR 83A; drive 1.3 miles and turn left on the signed road to the trailhead; drive 0.4 mile to the trailhead. *(The Forest Service map shows a different alignment for FR 24 than is actually on the ground. Follow this description and not the Forest Service map; the map is in the process of revision.)*

Fish Creek Canyon's steel-gray walls, with their strange spires and hoodoos chiseled by the elements, set the scene with an untamed feeling. Don't be too surprised if you encounter wildlife, such as bear, deer, or elk, instead of people.

The trail starts out on a steep downhill access trail to Fish Creek. A sunny section with slopes full of cobbles has **wild geranium, mullein,** and **Hooker's evening primrose** growing along the rocky sidelines. The more the trail drops, the more **red cinquefoil, Arizona rose,** and **Richardson's geranium** tag along. **Currant** line up along the trail as it turns a bend.

Cockerell's sedum, which normally prefers nestling in niches of rocky outcroppings, makes a brief show along the short ascent up a ridge. A colony of **yellow-eyed grass** waits on the ridgetop. Part of the iris family, these pale yellow flowers prefer the shade of coniferous forests. **Arizona peavine** and **birdsfoot morning glory** also mingle with the **yellow-eyed grass.**

Once the trail is on the downhill again, **mountain parsley** appears with **New Mexico locust** under a cover of ponderosa pines. The **New Mexico locust** usually flowers in June, but you can recognize the bush post-flower by its pinnately compound, rounded leaflets and the thorns on its branches and stems. When a stand of aspen appears, look for **brown-eyed Susan, yarrow,** and **Indian paintbrush** in the dapples of sun.

The trail arrives at the creek at mile 0.6 where a colony of **bergamot** cozies along a hedge of **red osier dogwood** and **osha. Poison ivy** likes the creekside, too, so watch carefully for the three-leaved plant throughout the hike. This makes a good turnaround point for a short day hike. To continue on this hike, turn right.

BROWN-EYED SUSAN
Rudbeckia laciniata

Brown-eyed Susan makes frequent appearances in the high country. The 3- to 6-foot-tall daisy likes rich forest soil and grows by mountain streams and cienegas. Since the flower has no browsers, it tends to flourish.

You can identify the yellow daisy from other members of the sunflower family by its large, deeply cut leaves. The leaves explain the plant's alternate name of cutleaf coneflower.

The trail makes its way through a forest of mixed conifers and aspen. **Richardson's geranium** and **cinquefoil** follow along the smooth, narrow path, passing **brown-eyed Susan** standing on the creekbanks and **bergamot** trailing along the path. In the shade of the aspens, **wood sorrel** surrounds a patch of **baneberry.**

Scouler's catchfly, Indian paintbrush, and **harebell** like the pockets of sun that dapple the wooded sections of trail. **Golden-beard penstemon** appear near creekcrossings which occur often throughout the hike. At about mile 1.5, **New Mexico checkermallow** finds a home in a spring that riffles across the trail. In a moist crook just beyond, watch for **verileaf phacelia** and **towering polemonium.**

At about mile 2, the canyon walls narrow briefly, becoming hanging gardens. The canyon opens back up quickly, however, and the trail alternates between stands of oaks and pines and grassy meadows. **Harebell** and **cinquefoil** dominate the meadows with touches of red from **Mexican silene** and **Indian paintbrush. Richardson's geranium** follows faithfully.

The trail climbs a sunny rise near mile 3 and brushes past a spread of electric-purple **verbena** and clusters of purple-tinged **plains beebalm.** The path stays above the creek awhile before dropping back down again.

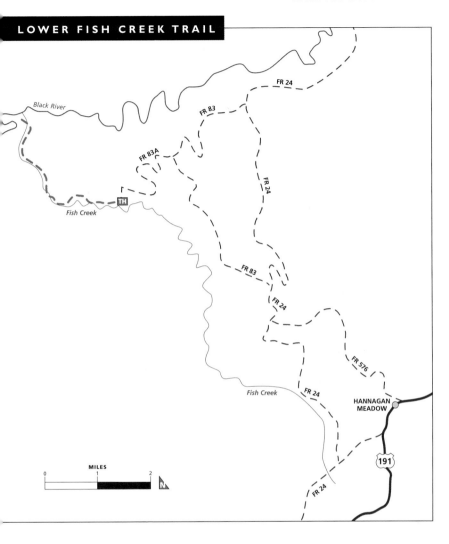

LOWER FISH CREEK TRAIL

At mile 3.6, you may smell a colony of the lily family's **nodding onion** as the trail enters an area splintered by a tornado years ago. Trees, yanked from the ground or snapped at their trunks, lie upon the canyon's slopes. This particularly sunny section brings **brown-eyed Susan** and **New Mexico checkermallow** to the creek's banks.

The trail gradually transitions from sun-filled meadow back to the cover of mixed conifers and intermittent clearings. Look for **larkspur** in the conifers and **shrubby cinquefoil** in the clearings. At a large clearing surrounded by ponderosa pines, mile 4.4, the trail passes through an old cowboy camp. Watch out for remnants of barbed wire around the camp.

The trail heads back into the conifers and its usual mix of botanicals. Be careful around mile 5, when the path brushes against several patches of **poison ivy** that encroach on the trail. Favoring disturbed areas, this irritating plant finds trailsides particularly alluring. The Black River, at trail's end, lies just beyond a primitive camp and gate. When you reach the river, return the way you came.

YELLOW-EYED GRASS
Sisyrinchium arizonicum

You may confuse yellow-eyed grass with Rocky Mountain iris if you don't see the plants in flower. They both belong to the iris family and have similar leaves. But Rocky Mountain iris's leaves are much longer and sword shaped, while yellow-eyed grass leaves are thinner and grasslike.

The flowers are completely different. The blue Rocky Mountain iris has three erect petals that form an unmistakable shape. Yellow-eyed grass has six pale-yellow pointed petals and three stamens with black tips. Also, Rocky Mountain iris prefers boggy areas, while yellow-eyed grass is comfortable in a mixed conifer forest.

South Fork Trail

Larkspur favor moist conditions found along the South Fork Trail.

The South Fork of the Little Colorado River sets the scene for its namesake hike with a riparian habitat that supports a wide variety of wildflowers. Fed by springs and runoff, the stream has a quick flow that barges through the landscape under the cover of alders, oaks, sycamores, and pines.

The South Fork Trail strings together a mix of shaded streamside habitats with sun-drenched meadows to produce a nonstop show of wildflowers. When the trail follows the stream closely, it displays many different moisture-loving plants, some unusual. When the trail veers into meadows, a multi-hued trove of flowers gathers around.

Trail Rating	Moderate
Trail Length	3.5 miles one way
Location	Eagar
Elevation	7,560–8,500 feet
Contact	Apache-Sitgreaves National Forest, Springerville Ranger District, 928-333-4372
Bloom Season	July–September
Peak Bloom	August
Directions	From Eagar drive west on AZ 260 about 7.4 miles to FR 560 (South Fork Road), and turn left (southwest); drive 2.7 miles to the trailhead.

The trail starts off in a meadow filled with a pleasing mix of color. Vibrant purples from **wild geranium** and **Lambert's locoweed** contrast with the gold from **cinquefoil** and **golden aster**. **Many-flowered gromwell's** clusters of yellow funnel flowers and rayless **large-flowered brickellbush** appear around **Arizona rose**. **Gray's lousewort** rises above spreads of **poison ivy**. **Skyrocket** tosses a red-orange burst of blossoms past **Mexican hat** daisies.

The trail comes close to the South Fork at about mile 0.25. If you take one of the short footpaths to the water, you may see white umbels on **wild celery, osha,** or **Douglas' water hemlock**. At first blush, these wildflowers look alike. If you look closer, their leaf structures tell them apart. Another important, and hidden, difference: **hemlock** is poisonous!

The mass of red-stemmed bushes the trail passes at mile 0.3 is **red-osier dogwood**. Usually creekside dwellers, these bushes expanded their territory during times of high water. Watch for **virgin's bower** vine twisting in the bushes and **black medick** carpeting the trailsides.

After climbing out of the constraints of the canyon, the trail edges an eroded slope. **Wright's deervetch** and **groundsel** hold tightly onto the water-sloughed hillside. Sunshine draws **Mexican woollywhite** and **antelope sage**.

At about mile 0.4, the trail heads back into the trees, staying several feet above the drainage. The loose-knit cover of ponderosa pines provides enough sun to load the trailsides with wildflowers. Some areas feature **cinquefoil**, others **larkspur**, and others **western dayflower** or **western blue flax**. **Skyrocket** provides occasional bursts. Thickets of **Arizona rose** grow in clusters. And **princely daisy** makes a frequent show. Watch, too, for **red cinquefoil** and white daisies with purple undersides called **tower daisy**.

The trail and the creek meet on common ground around mile 1. **Red cinquefoil** and **larkspur** like the moist environment. Then the trail climbs out of the drainage at mile 1.1 and resumes its flower-speckled dapples-of-sun routine as it continues under the cover of pines. Check for **amber lily, Mexican silene, bergamot,** and **spreading four o'clock.**

The trail has another close encounter with the creek at about mile 1.9, which attracts **larkspur** and **tower daisy. Richardson's geranium** and **harebell** line the trail's edges. On the trail's climb out of the drainage, look for **elegant camus,** another poisonous plant, and **foothill kittentails.** The large, sprawling evergreen just before the trail crosses a primitive road at about mile 2 is a common juniper. After crossing the road, continue straight.

Keeping close to the creek, the trail often draws moisture-loving plants to its sides. **Bergamot** spreads purple colonies in the tall grasses along the trail, and **larkspur** raises its royal blue flowers above them. **New Mexico vervain** lifts its purple clusters above the field, too.

The trail crosses the creek at about mile 2.4. Nonpoisonous **osha** mixes with **spotted water hemlock,** another extremely poisonous plant. The **hemlock's** inflorescence and purple-streaked stem is what differentiates it from **osha.** A few steps farther, the trail comes to a fork where you veer right.

Antelope sage whitens the canyon slope on the left, and **wild geranium, western dayflower, Mexican silene,** and **skyrocket** color the trailsides. After passing through a gate at mile 2.6 (be sure to latch the gate), the trail climbs up the canyonslope briefly, then heads down into a wetland filled with **larkspur.** Next, the trail enters a long meadow dotted pink with **mountain thistle.** Look for a colony of **western blue flax** along the west side of the trail, and **heal all** blooming under the grasses on the east side.

The trail rambles through a string of meadows as it heads to its end at mile 3.5. **Lambert's locoweed, silver-stem lupine,** and **larkspur** form blue pools of flowers. **Cinquefoil** lays spreads of yellow and

WESTERN BLUE FLAX
Linum lewisii

The blue saucer-shaped flowers on western blue flax produce an ethereal display along a high country trail. But you need to catch the blossoms during the morning hours, because they usually drop their petals by the afternoon. Western blue flax favors ponderosa clearings and roadsides.

The stem of the plant contains the long fibers so characteristic of flax. If you twist the stem, it will not readily break and has a twinelike consistency.

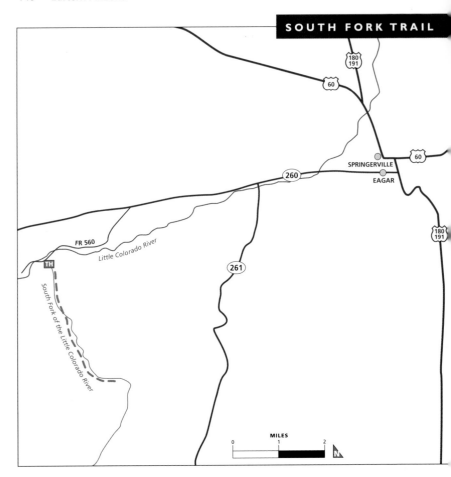

pink windmill tops gangly stems. You most likely will see elk tracks in these meadows, and possibly bear tracks.

The hike ends at a wide fork in the creek, an idyllic spot where **crimson monkey flower** jewels the water, **cow clover** outlines the stream edges, and **New Mexico checkermallow** stands with **Franciscan bluebell** on the banks. **Osha** sends up white umbels next to the gold daisy flowers of **brown-eyed Susan**. A colony of **bergamot** stands off to the side. Return the way you came.

Steeple Trail

A gathering of false hellebore creates a moody atmosphere.

The Steeple Trail will take you all the way to the Blue River if you choose. In the 13 miles it travels to the Blue, the trail passes through mixed conifer-aspen forests, squishes across cienegas, ducks under a riparian forest, and finally finishes in a piñon-juniper forest punctuated with cactus.

This hike, however, stays in an alpine environment, passing through forests, along streams, and in cienegas with a large variety of botanicals in the different environments. The remote areas the trail covers are frequented by elk, bear, deer, and Mexican gray wolves. As wild as the area can get, the trail still retains a comfortable demeanor.

Trail Rating	Moderate
Trail Length	2.8 miles
Location	Alpine
Elevation	9,040–9,200 feet
Contact	Apache-Sitgreaves National Forest, Alpine Ranger District, 928-339-4384
Bloom Season	July–September
Peak Bloom	August
Special Considerations	This trail is located in the Blue Range Primitive Area where no mechanized vehicles, including mountain bikes, are allowed.
	Parts of the Steeple Trail are located in the Mexican gray wolf recovery area and may be closed because of denning. Check with the Forest Service for trail status.
Directions	From Alpine, drive south on US 191 about 23 miles to the signed turnoff (across from Hannagan Meadow), and turn left (east); drive 0.4 mile to the trailhead parking area.

The trail starts in an aspen-fir forest that is carpeted with **bracken fern.** **Sneezeweed** springs up in answer to rays of sunlight allowed in pockets. **Bracted strawberry, mountain parsley,** and **Richardson's geranium,** usually faithful in low-light landscapes, appear with **Canada violet** and early-blooming **elkslip.** Watch for **Scouler's catchfly** and **Indian paintbrush.**

The trail bends into a spread of **thermopsis** edged by **Franciscan bluebell.** The **thermopsis** blooms yellow pea flowers in the spring, and may also have remnant seedpods from the blooms. **Wood sorrel, harebell,** and **sweet Cicely** fill in the gaps. The **thermopsis** has its way until about mile 0.5 when a lowland clearing brings in **silver-stem lupine** and another springtime bloomer, **Rocky Mountain iris.**

Brown-eyed Susan gathers in a trailside cienega that develops into a stream as it travels down a V-shaped drainage next to the trail. By mile 1, the trail sinks into the wetland. A jumble of **New Mexico checkermallow, false hellebore, brown-eyed Susan, osha,** and **Franciscan bluebell** crowd around the trail, which, during wet weather, becomes a drainage. **Cow clover** and **heal all** spread along the streamside.

The stream veers across the trail to the path's other side with botanicals in tow. Look for **monkshood** here. These distinctive deep-blue flowers stand several feet tall, rubbing shoulders with **false hellebore** and **osha.**

At mile 1.3, the trail drops into a cienega where it meets the Upper Grant Creek Trail (see p. 153). Lichen drips from conifers circling the cienega, and islands of **Rocky Mountain iris** mottle the cienega. **Mouse-ear chickweed** and **wood sorrel** mix with long grasses, while **harebell, Whipple's penstemon, mountain lobelia,** and **Wright's bluets** add speckles of color.

The trail climbs out of the cienega and edges another stream heading down to the cienega. **Silver-stem lupine** looks down from the trail's upslope. The stream gurgles from beneath a cover of **wood sorrel** and **heal all. Franciscan bluebell, hellebore,** and **brown-eyed Susan** line the stream. In a sunny stretch, about mile 1.5, **spur gentian, nodding groundsel,** and **Scouler's catchfly** mix with the streamside botanicals. Also watch for **buttercup** before the trail pulls away from the stream and enters a forest, at about mile 1.6.

A couple of flower-filled clearings break up the forest until about mile 1.8. Then the trail stays in the forest as it contours the large meadow in which Willow Spring is located. Watch for **mouse-ear chickweed** and **verileaf phacelia** between colonies of **thermopsis** and **silver-leaf lupine** in small meadows.

Also watch for **giant rattlesnake plantain** and **adder's mouth.** Both of these wildflowers belong to the orchid family. **Giant rattlesnake plantain** has an elongated cluster of tiny white flowers, and **adder's mouth** has a green cluster. **Adder's mouth** grows from a corm, which looks like the hip joint on a chicken bone.

The trail leaves the meadows behind at about mile 2.2 and starts a long climb up a ridge, heading into the thick of a forest. Shadow-lovers like **giant rattlesnake plantain, death camas, Canada violet,** and **slender bog orchid** come to the trailside. **Elkslip** practically forms a groundcover. **Thimbleberry** shows fragile raspberrylike fruit. Mosses upholster deadfall and boulders, and trees are shaggy with lichen.

FALSE HELLEBORE
Veratrum californicum

If you stand in a colony of false hellebore, you might find yourself looking up at their green-tinged clusters of star-shaped flowers. The plant usually stands 3 to 6 feet tall, and can reach 8 feet. And you'll probably have to get your feet wet if you mingle among them. They dwell around mountain streams and cienegas. You can easily recognize false hellebore by its stalk of heavily veined cornlike leaves.

This plant contains several alkaloids that slow the heartbeat and lower blood pressure. Indian and Anglo herbalists during colonial times used false hellebore for these features. Today, most herbalists discourage its use because incorrect doses cause death.

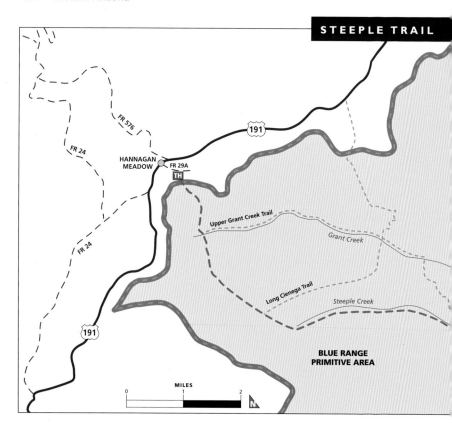

At about mile 2.6, the trail starts its drop to Long Cienega, a large wetland full of **Rocky Mountain iris**. As the trail crosses the spongy ground, **silver-stem lupine, Whipple's penstemon, harebell, cinquefoil,** and **yarrow** color the grasses. A colony of **Indian paintbrush** hangs out near a small stand of aspen.

You may continue on the Steeple Trail, create a loop with the Long Cienega and Upper Grant Creek Trails back to the Steeple Trail, or return the way you came. If you take the Long Cienega Trail, the Forest Service labels the trail as primitive. The trail may require route-finding skills as downfall and overgrowth often mask the path.

Upper Grant Creek Trail

Creeksides get thick with flowers and berries on the Upper Grant Creek Trail.

This hike starts on the Steeple Trail (see p. 149) and follows it 1.3 miles to a cienega and the start of the Upper Grant Creek Trail. Turn left onto the Upper Grant Creek Trail to continue on this hike.

The trail slogs through the cienega to Grant Creek and follows the watercourse as it tumbles down a wooded canyon. The creekside hike takes you through a remote section of the Blue Range Primitive Area where cowboys worked and moonshiners hid in years gone by, where bears grub around downfall and Mexican gray wolves roam, and where dozens of different wildflowers fill creekbanks and line trailsides.

As you hike through the spongy ground of the cienega, **wood sorrel** fills in where **thermopsis** and **Rocky Mountain iris** (both spring

Trail Rating	Strenuous
Trail Length	5.3 miles one way
Location	Alpine
Elevation	7,120–9,200 feet
Contact	Apache-Sitgreaves National Forest, Alpine Ranger District, 928-339-4384
Bloom Season	July–September
Peak Bloom	August
Special Considerations	This trail is located in the Blue Range Primitive Area where no mechanized vehicles, including mountain bikes, are allowed. Parts of the Upper Grant Creek Trail are located in the Mexican gray wolf recovery area and may be closed because of denning. Check with the Forest Service for trail status.
Directions	From Alpine, drive south on US 191 about 23 miles to the signed turnoff (across from Hannagan Meadow), and turn left (east). Drive 0.4 mile to the trailhead parking area.

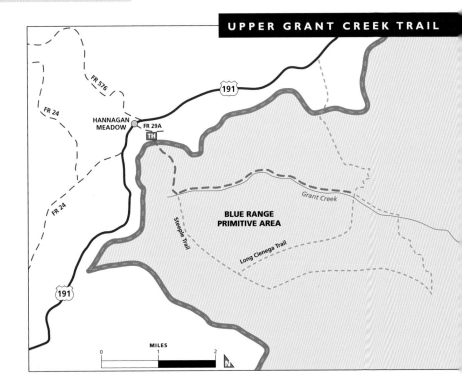

UPPER GRANT CREEK TRAIL

FR 576

191

FR 24

HANNAGAN MEADOW

FR 29A

TH

FR 24

191

Steeple Trail

Grant Creek

BLUE RANGE PRIMITIVE AREA

Long Cienega Trail

MILES

0   1   2

N

bloomers) don't grow. **Brown-eyed Susan** lifts gold daisies over the green cover. The trail slices right through the **thermopsis** into a fir-aspen forest. **Canada violet** and **thimbleberry** mix with moss-covered rocks that edge the path.

The trail enters a sumptuous area at the first of many streamcrossings when it passes **red elderberry, bracted strawberry,** and **currant** bushes. **Franciscan bluebell** cascades from a natural pile of rocks near the creek, and **osha** lines up on the banks.

The trail varies between color along the trailsides from **wild geranium, Mexican silene,** and **plains beebalm** and pretty creekside scenes filled with **osha, lady fern, brown-eyed Susan,** and **false hellebore.** Then the trail goes into shadows where **sweet Cicely, thimbleberry,** and **Canada violet** feel comfortable.

At mile 1.8, the creek makes a braided flow through fragmented pieces of land. **New Mexico checkermallow** hugs the stepping-stone–sized islands. Between the next quick creekcrossings, the trailsides become moist enough for **polemonium** and **red cinquefoil.** At a rocky seep, about mile 2, watch for **Cockerell's sedum** nesting in the rocks.

The forest opens up a bit, and the extra sunlight cultivates a thicket of **Arizona rose** pocketed with **Hooker's evening primrose.** Be careful of **poison ivy** in this area.

At about mile 2.25, the trail may ooze with ephemeral springs during wet weather. This makes a favorable habitat for **monkshood.** You may spot the deep-blue hooded flower nodding over the creek with **red figwort** and **brown-eyed Susan. Alumroot** takes advantage of loamy growth on the rocks along the trail in this area and in the weeping rock wall the trail passes at mile 2.5. Water drips down a shaggy travertine of moss and minerals forming on the wall. **Sweet Cicely** and **baneberry** grow along the rock wall's base, a lovely contrast to the green moss.

ARIZONA ROSE
Rosa arizonica

There are two species of wild rose in Arizona: Arizona rose and Fendler rose. The easiest way to identify them is by their thorns. Arizona rose has thick, curved thorns and the Fendler rose has thinner and straighter thorns. Arizona rose only grows to about 3 feet, while Fendler rose grows three times larger and has a bigger blossom.

The tangy-tasting fruit of the rose bushes, called hips, often lingers on their branches through the winter. You can pluck the fruit right off the bush and eat it. The hips contain relatively high amounts of vitamins C and A.

The trail dries out by mile 2.9, keeping to the north side of the creek for a while. **Mountain lover** joins the forest floor cover of **bracted strawberry, Richardson's geranium,** and **thimbleberry. Mountain parsley** and **Scouler's catchfly** make occasional appearances with **aspen fleabane. Bergamot** appears at about mile 3.7, when the trail starts to make creekcrossings again. Some of these crossings can turn into a project if you want to keep your feet dry.

The trail begins a pattern of climbing over the creekbed and traveling on high ground between crossings where **skyrocket, Fendler's ceanothus,** and **golden-beard penstemon** hang out. During this stretch, the creek drops considerably in elevation. The wildflowers that gathered at the creekcrossings in the higher elevations are replaced by **red-osier dogwood** and **poison ivy** the size of small trees.

At mile 4.8, the trail arrives at a moonshiner's cabin and corral where copper moonshine equipment was found. **Spreading four o'clock** and **western dayflower** add color to the shadowed site.

The trail joins the Grant Cabin Trail at mile 4.9, and the Long Cienega Trail at mile 5.1. You may continue to the trail's end at the Paradise Trail at mile 5.3 and return the way you came or loop back to the Steeple Trail on the Long Cienega Trail.

Wild four o'clock blossoms intertwined with an agave.

Thompson Trail

Meadows along the Thompson Trail are filled with flowers.

The trail begins near the Thompson Ranch on an old road now closed to all but foot traffic. Following the West Fork of the Black River, a nationally recognized blue ribbon fishery, the trail shows off dozens of different wildflowers along the meadowed canyon floor, surrounded by mixed conifers and stands of aspens.

From its start, **yarrow, spreading four o'clock, wild geranium, Hooker's evening primrose, harebell, cinquefoil,** and **bigleaf avens** appear. Most of these wildflowers stick with the trail.

Several avalanches of gray boulders have tumbled down the canyon walls and into the river. At the first one, a quarter mile down the trail, look for **Cockerell's sedum** and **towering polemonium** growing upon

Trail Rating	Easy
Trail Length	2.5 miles one way
Location	Eagar
Elevation	8,600–8,840 feet
Contact	Apache-Sitgreaves National Forest, Springerville Ranger District, 928-333-4372
Bloom Season	July–September
Peak Bloom	August
Special Considerations	Trail is open to foot travel only.
Directions	From Eagar, drive 3 miles west on AZ 260 and turn left (south) onto AZ 261. Drive 17 miles to Crescent Lake and turn right (west) onto FR 113; drive about 2.5 miles to FR 116 and turn left (south). Drive about 4 miles to the trailhead.

THOMPSON TRAIL

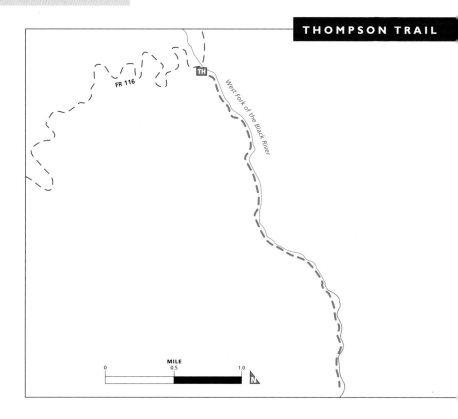

and among the rocks. **Western bistort** displays white clusters of flowers on leafless stems. **Sneezeweed** clusters around the creek, and **Geyer's onion's** grasslike leaves release a telltale onion smell.

Just past the avalanche debris, you start to see **Franciscan bluebell, New Mexico checkermallow,** and dainty **Nuttall's linanthus. Shrubby cinquefoil** is often snuggled right next to the boulders.

At mile 0.5, the trail passes a dam erected to keep rainbow trout from spawning up the creek. An old railroad bed is located just upslope from the trail, and several paths lead up to it during the course of the trail. Mountain bikes and horses are allowed to ride on this raised path, which parallels the Thompson Trail most of the way. To stay on the Thompson Trail, veer left toward the creek.

The trail continues through a gate and enters a wooded section. **Plains beebalm, red raspberry,** and **fireweed** appear right away in the filtered sunlight. Just down the path, **mountain parsley, dwarf goldenrod,** and **large-flowered brickellbush** line up on the trail's outside slope. **Bracted strawberry** and **meadow rue** take to the shadows.

At a second dam, you might get your feet wet in a bog where **Rocky Mountain iris** thrives. Stepping-stones help you navigate through this spongy area and other boggy stretches that appear during wet weather along the trail.

At about mile 1, the trail leaves the boggy area and heads toward a dry meadow where **verileaf phacelia** hangs out. **Indian paintbrush** adds a sprinkling of color in the meadow. Around a bend, watch for **western bistort** to return at another bog. **Western bistort** has astringent properties. A poultice of the curved rootstock is said to stop the bleeding of a wound.

As the trail climbs up a scattering of jagged boulders,

SCOULER'S CATCHFLY
Silene scouleri

Scouler's catchfly may be the most curious member of the pink family. In starburst fashion, deeply lobed, slender mauve petals surround a small inset of lighter-colored petals. This setup extends from a distended calyx described by some as a miniature striped watermelon. This calyx makes Scouler's catchfly distinctive even when wilted.

The sticky and hairy Scouler's catchfly makes a regular appearance in moist forests. The plant's stickiness protects it from predator insects.

wild chrysanthemum start to edge the trail. Look for a small colony of **green gentian** across the creek. Once past the rocky section, the trail crosses a hillside full of **skyrocket** that add a soft red-orange hue, then heads back down to the creek as the waterway bends to the east.

Right away, the squat stalks of yellow **Mogollon Indian paintbrush** — its only appearance along the trail—grabs your attention as the trail enters a wide meadow. Watch for **Scouler's catchfly** where the trail flirts with some spruce trees, and **western blue flax** just beyond.

At about mile 2, the trail pulls away from the creek briefly, then rejoins it in a field carpeted with **fleabane**. At trail's end, look for **Parry pedicularis**. Return the way you came.

Rocky Mountain Iris

West Baldy Trail

Wildflower Hike 34

The West Fork of the Little Colorado River draws a lot of wildflowers wherever it goes.

The West Baldy Trail, a full 7 miles long, climbs nearly to the top of Mount Baldy, Arizona's second highest peak. The mountaintop is sacred to the Apache Indians and lies in the White Mountain Apache Reservation. Hikers must have a permit to climb to its top, beyond the trail's fenced end. No permits are needed for the West Baldy Trail hike, however, as it merely follows the creek in alpine meadows that foster an abundance of wildflowers.

Yarrow and harebell gather around the start of the trail as it makes its way through a gate into a loose mix of conifers that provides a matrix of shade in a sunny meadow. **Evening primrose** and **cinquefoil** weave in yellow. **Wild geranium, mountain parsley,** and **white prairie clover** appear when the trees gather along the trail.

Trail Rating	Easy (first 1.7 miles)—strenuous
Trail Length	1.5–7 miles one way
Location	Show Low
Elevation	9,000–9,400 feet
Contact	Apache-Sitgreaves National Forest, Springerville Ranger District, 928-333-4372
Bloom Season	July–September
Peak Bloom	August
Special Considerations	Most of this trail lies in the Mount Baldy Wilderness where mechanized vehicles, including mountain bikes, are not allowed.
Directions	From Show Low, drive southeast about 30 miles on AZ 260 and turn right (south) on AZ 273 (this becomes FR 113 south of Sunrise Lake); drive about 9 miles to the trailhead.

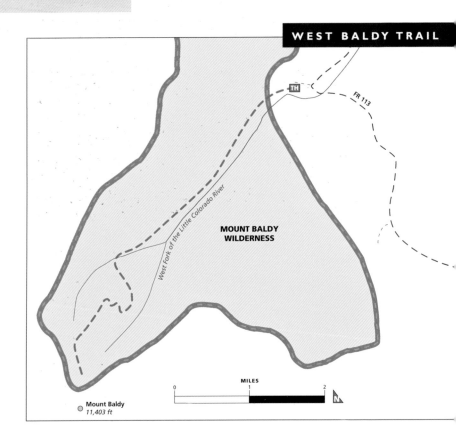

WEST BALDY TRAIL

FR 113

West Fork of the Little Colorado River

MOUNT BALDY WILDERNESS

MILES

0   1   2

N

Mount Baldy
11,403 ft

When the trail bends to the left onto an old road, watch for pink **skyrocket**, not a typical color for the often red-orange flower. Within a short distance, the trail bends again to the left onto a single track that drops gently into a vale harboring **Rocky Mountain iris**, then quickly climbs out into stands of mixed conifers and aspens. The iris blooms in the springtime and animals usually steer clear of its thick clumps of tough leaves. **Spur gentian** and **Indian paintbrush** bask in sunny patches between the stands.

After the trail passes through a second gate, the forest thickens and shade prevails, but dapples of sun coax **mouse-ear chickweed** and **Scouler's catchfly** along the trail. Eventually the clearings come back, and in them **trailing four o'clock, green gentian**, and budlike clusters of purple **pleated gentian.**

Members of the gentian family tend to have medicinal properties, and many are used as a tonic to help cleanse the blood and aid digestion. **Green gentian**, described by its scientific name of *speciosa*, meaning "showy," has roots with emetic properties.

Once again the trail starts a gradual descent, this time down to the West Fork drainage that meanders in a wide meadow soaked in sun. Most all of the wildflowers that collected in earlier clearings also converge here. On an old snag lying near a split-rail fence along the trail, you may see **red raspberry** bushes displaying their fruit. If you take a look along the river, you may see **New Mexico checkermallow, false hellebore, larkspur, osha**, and **Franciscan bluebell** among the colonies of **sneezeweed.**

More **Rocky Mountain iris** show up at the Mount Baldy Wilderness boundary sign, about mile 1. As the trail continues, look for **shrubby cinquefoil**, which likes to gather around boulders scattered in the meadow. When the terrain squeezes the trail and West Fork closer, **baneberry** and **Canada violet** gather by the path.

Soon the trail starts its hard climb up the mountain, going from alpine meadow to wooded slopes. This is a good turnaround point. Return the way you came. However, you may continue to almost the top of Mount Baldy.

NEW MEXICO CHECKERMALLOW

Sidalcea neomexicana

New Mexico checkermallow does not appear frequently around the state. You most often find its pretty pink clusters of flowers around the edge of a mountain stream or in wet meadows. The plant displays two shapes of leaves: round scalloped leaves on the lower part of the plant and deeply lobed ones on the upper part of the plant. Indians used to eat the leaves as greens.

Wildflower Hike 35 *East Baldy Trail*

The East Fork of the Little Colorado River nurtures rich displays of wildflowers along the East Baldy Trail.

Trail Rating	Easy (first 0.75 mile)—strenuous
Trail Length	0.75–7 miles one way
Location	Show Low
Elevation	9,300–9,400 feet
Contact	Apache-Sitgreaves National Forest, Springerville Ranger District, 928-333-4372
Bloom Season	July–September
Peak Bloom	August
Special Considerations	Most of this trail lies in the Mount Baldy Wilderness where mechanized vehicles, including mountain bikes, are not allowed.
Directions	From Show Low, drive southeast about 30 miles on AZ 260 and turn right (south) on AZ 273 (which becomes FR 113 south of Sunrise Lake); drive 11.3 miles to the signed trailhead.

The East Baldy Trail, like the popular West Baldy Trail (see p. 161), eventually makes its way 7 miles nearly to the top of Mount Baldy. This alternate route, however, attracts less of a crowd. The trail follows the East Fork of the Little Colorado River through a long meadow, then starts an extreme climb up the mountain. This hike takes you 0.75 mile through meadowland along the creek, staying well out of the way of excessive climbing, but right in the heart of the trail's cache of wildflowers.

Before the trail leaves the parking area, check out an island of aspen and spruce trees in the parking area. **Gray's lousewort** sends up towering fern-leaved stalks with elongated clusters of two-lipped flowers. The flowers appear to be a rose color, but actually are yellow with red-brown lines. **Whipple's penstemon** spreads along the edges of the little island.

On the trail, in a meadow edged by an aspen-spruce forest, you see a variety of flowers woven in with the grass. **Cinquefoil** spreads flecks of gold across the landscape. **Princely daisy** raises single purple daisies with thread-thin petals. **Harebell** sprinkles in rich blue blossoms. **Scouler's catchfly** shows distinctive dusty-pink flower heads that look like a sunburst at the end of a swollen calyx.

Orange agoseris, which goes by the nickname of orange mountain dandelion, makes attractive appearances. Both agoseris and dandelion belong to the sunflower family and have milky stem juice.

FIREWEED
Epilobium angustifolium

When fireweed bursts on the scene, you can't help but notice its magenta clusters of flowers that grow up to 6 feet tall. The plant likes disturbed places, especially burn areas where it covers the charred land in droves. This propensity gives the plant its common name.

The plant gets its scientific name from its leaves. *Angustifolium* means *narrow-leaved*. Narrow and lance-shaped, the leaves' veins form a scalloped pattern near their edges. The plant's distinctive pink flowers look like its cousins in the evening primrose family—each petal stands on its own, separated to the base.

Like its cousins, fireweed produces a pod. The tiny seeds inside have a tuft of silky hairs attached. When the pod opens, the silken hairs keep the seeds adrift on the wind so they can disperse.

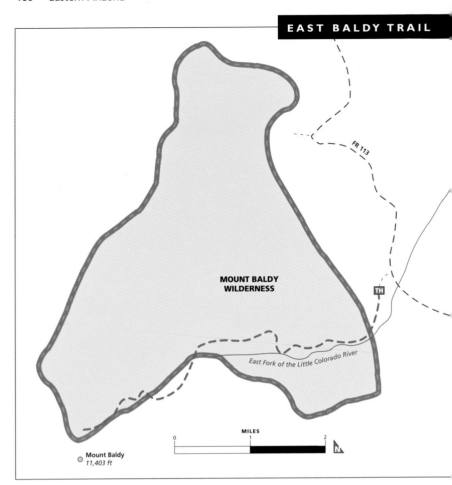

FR 113

MOUNT BALDY
WILDERNESS

TH

East Fork of the Little Colorado River

MILES

0   1   2

Mount Baldy
11,403 ft

The treeline moves closer as the trail heads toward the creek. You might even see a herd of elk grazing on the forest's edge.

By about mile 0.3, the path comes creekside to a new variety of flowers. **Osha** opens white umbels along the banks, and attention-getting stalks of **false hellebore** grow up to 8 feet tall. **Franciscan bluebell** arches over the stream. **Shrubby cinquefoil** lays low to the ground, often embracing small boulders. **Cow clover** spreads right along the banks.

You may smell **field mint** as you peruse the creekbanks. The foot-high plants with pink clusters of flowers emit a strong mint scent, especially when brushed against or stepped upon. Like most mints, the **field mint** provides mint flavoring and aids in digestion.

The trail heads southwest along the creek. The meadow on the north side continues with familiar flowers: **orange agoseris, harebell, Scouler's catchfly,** and **cinquefoil**. Also watch for **aspen fleabane**, which looks similar to the **princely daisy**, but with several flowers on a stem, and **tower daisy**, a single-flower daisy that has purple undersides to its white petals.

You may also see fly agaric mushrooms with their distinguishing red caps speckled with uneven raised white dots. Extremely attractive and poisonous, the mushroom got its name from a concoction (made by steeping the mushroom in milk) that stupefies flies. The North American fly agaric mushrooms do not produce visions in humans, only delirium, raving, and profuse sweating.

Just before a fork in the trail, watch for an errant avalanche of jagged boulders piled near the creek. The gray basalt boulders have colorful mottles of chartreuse-colored lichen, an attractive scene. You may find magenta clusters of **fireweed**, powder-blue **Franciscan bluebell**, white **plains beebalm**, and chubby yellow **nodding groundsel** in the jumble of rock. **Dwarf goldenrod** watches from the trailsides.

At the fork in the trail, veer left to stay near the creek. **Orange agoseris** increases in the meadow, **buttercup** shows up near the creek, and **willow weed** stands right along the creek's banks. Watch for **Mexican woollywhite** on the upslope of the trail.

Just before the creekside path rejoins the trail, look for a colony of **hooded ladies' tresses**. The plant, part of the orchid family, has three spiraled rows of white flowers. Also watch for **spur gentian** on either side of the path.

When the path rejoins the trail, you may continue on the East Baldy Trail, or return the way you came.

Wildflower Hike 36 ## Butler Canyon Nature Trail

Colorful groups of wildflowers and mushrooms are found along the Butler Canyon Nature Trail.

This nature trail takes you through several different environments you may experience while hiking in the White Mountains, such as a moist mixed conifer forest, sunny meadows, fertile streamcrossings, and a pine forest. Each has its own particular accompaniment of wildflowers.

The hike starts in a meadow crowded with **cinquefoil, Lambert's loco-weed, yarrow,** and **princely daisy.** A colony of **silver-stem lupine** gathers at the trailhead sign. Look for **Gray's lousewort** just across the trail from the sign. The tall, fern-leaved plant sometimes blends in with trailside brush because its cluster of flowers—yellow with reddish lines—have a subdued rosy color. The Latin name *Pedicularis* means louse. The name comes from

Trail Rating	Easy
Trail Length	1-mile loop
Location	Greer
Elevation	8,000–8,100 feet
Contact	Apache-Sitgreaves National Forest, Springerville Ranger District, 928-333-4372
Bloom Season	July–September
Peak Bloom	August
Directions	From Eagar, go west on AZ 260 12 miles to the intersection of AZ 260 and AZ 373. Turn left (south) on AZ 373 and go 4.1 miles to Greer. Turn left (east) on East Fork Road/FR 8079 and drive 0.1 mile to the signed trailhead.

a superstition that claimed cattle would have more lice if they ate these plants. **Gray's lousewort** appears in moist, forested areas along the trail.

On the way to a sign requesting hikers not to smoke along the trail, **tower daisy** mixes with **Scouler's catchfly**, **Arizona rose**, and **Mexican woolly-white**. **Tower daisy** has a purple underside on its petals, which distinguishes it from the handful of other daisy flowers along the path.

A small stand of trees provides enough shade for **false Solomon's seal**, **Canada violet**, and **meadow rue** to feel comfortable. **Golden-beard penstemon** and **wild geranium** add bits of red and purple color where the sun hits. The shadow-lovers persist with the trail into an aspen-fir forest, and **Richardson's geranium** joins up with them. Look for **Gray's lousewort** near a sign with a trail icon of a bear paw and a nearby colony of **Arizona rose**. The rose bushes' fragrant flowers bloom in June, and you may see their hips by August.

Woodland pinedrops and **foothill kittentails** like this moist environment, and you can find them mixing with **bracken fern**. **Woodland pinedrops**, a saprophyte, often stands inconspicuously in colonies of ferns and plants. **Foothill kittentails** have a column of pink blossoms that are more green bract than pink petals and sometimes hard to spot. But once you do, you can easily identify them by their blossom design and hairy leaves tinged with red.

Dapples of sunlight draw **harebell**, **Scouler's catchfly**, **silver-stem lupine**, and **princely daisy** into the forest. **Star Solomon's seal** gathers in colonies along the trail.

The forest dwellers continue with the path as it climbs a mild slope. Below the trail to the left, a cover of **bracken fern** hides a stream feeding **false hellebore** and **osha**. The tall blue-flowered plants are **monkshood**, and the red-berried bushes are **baneberry**. When the trail levels out, you may see **many-flowered gromwell** and **Indian paintbrush** in a flurry of **princely daisy**. Watch for a lone **twinberry** bush nesting near a log on the south side of the trail.

Lambert's **locoweed** edges the trail as it enters a ponderosa park where sunshine coaxes a colony of **sneezeweed** to infiltrate the **bracken fern** below. The trail rounds a bend enveloping a meadow full of flowers and then it heads for the drainage, passing common juniper bushes on the left.

A variety of wildflowers pack themselves into the drainage. **Richardson's geranium** fills the spaces between **false hellebore**. Tall **tansy mustard** sends up candelabras of branches with small yellow clusters. **Monkshood** lines up in the background. Pretty pink **New Mexico checkermallow** melds with yellow daisy **brown-eyed Susan**.

The trail crosses a bridge, and then another next to a thicket of **twinberry** and **Arizona rose** bushes, then continues through a flower-filled meadow to a cool spring. **Skyrocket, yarrow, harebell**, and **silver-stem lupine** color the meadow. After crossing a road, the path climbs another mild slope into a field spread with the same flowers, plus **wild chrysanthemum, spreading four o'clock**, and **Mexican silene**.

As the path rounds to the north face of a slope, away from water

MONKSHOOD
Aconitum columbianum

Displaying the same beautiful flower color and plant size, monkshood and larkspur are often confused. The monkshood's trademark helmet-shaped sepal, said to resemble a hood worn by medieval monks, helps delineate it from the larkspur, which has a tapering spur instead.

Like larkspur, monkshood has front petals that must be pushed back by a pollinator in order for it to enter the helmet of the flower where the nectar lies. If you look inside the helmet with a magnifier, you can see fine white hairs around the inner edge of the flower's mouth. Just behind the hairs lie a tangle of anthers.

Monkshood also goes by the name of wolfbane. The name comes from its folklore use in warding away the notorious werewolf.

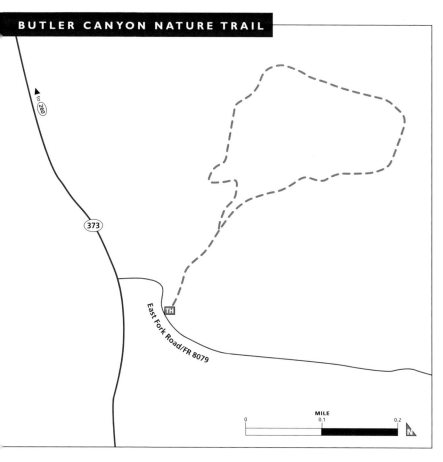

and full sun, the flowers diminish. Lichen-mottled outcroppings rise along the trail where **large-flowered brickellbush** likes to hang out. As the trail drops back down toward the trailhead and into the sunshine, **princely daisy** gathers with **Lambert's locoweed, cinquefoil,** and **Mexican woollywhite.** The trail makes one last streamcrossing just before coming full circle, and gives you a close-up look at **monkshood** and **Gray's lousewort.** Watch for **agrimonia** and **Franciscan bluebell,** too.

*Wildflower
Hike 37* ## Ash Creek Trail

*Wildflowers like
to congregate
along the banks
of Ash Creek.*

The Pinaleno Mountains, a range sacred to the Apache Indians, got their name from a tribe of Indians who lived in the mountains and called themselves the Piñon Lanos. Later, an 1851 Sitgreaves map corrected the spelling to Pinal Llano, Spanish for Pine Plain. The name wrangled its way to the present name.

The mountains also once went by the apropos name of Sierra Bonita, Spanish for "beautiful mountain." The Ash Creek Trail, one of the prettier trails in the range, follows Ash Creek down the north face of the mountain to the desert floor. In the summer, the upper 2.5 miles of the trail make an excellent wildflower hike.

Trail Rating	Strenuous
Trail Length	2.5 miles one way
Location	Safford, Mount Graham
Elevation	8,200–9,490 feet
Contact	Coronado National Forest, Safford Ranger District, 928-428-4150
Bloom Season	July–September
Peak Bloom	August
Directions	From Safford, take US 191 south about 7 miles to AZ 366. Turn right (southwest) and drive about 7 miles (AZ 366 ends and becomes Swift Trail road). Continue another 22 miles on the winding Swift Trail road to the trailhead.

The trail starts in a forest of aspen and Douglas fir, but soon opens into a small clearing with **purple vetch** mounding on the ground around colonies of **false hellebore** and **cow parsnip**. Both of these plants have a tall stature and distinctive leaves. The **false hellebore**, which also goes by the name of corn lily, has leaves similar to corn and is poisonous. **Cow parsnip**, easily identified with or without its white umbels because of its coarsely-toothed leaves, provides food for elk and black bear.

Shortly after re-entering the woods, the trail passes the ruins of a log shack associated with a sawmill that operated near Ash Creek Falls during the 1930s. The path starts a zigzag down to the intersection with the Webb Peak Trail. Shadow-loving **Canada violet** and **wild geranium** gather around a rusty piece of machinery left behind from the sawmill at the intersection. **Bracken fern** spreads on the forest floor.

The trail meets up with Ash Creek at about mile 0.7 and begins to follow the perennial stream down the mountain. This sunny section of trail provokes a rich meeting of flowers along the creek. Watch how **osha** squeezes among the statuesque **false hellebore** and **cow parsnip** along the water's edge. **Franciscan bluebell** dangles elongated clusters of blue bell flowers over the creek. **Yellow columbine** bows lanky stems on the creekbanks green with **thimbleberry** and **baneberry**. Look for the white **shooting star**, unusual in color and is uncommon to this area.

After another creekcrossing, the trail leaves these flowers behind and rises above the creek. Spotty showings of **mountain ninebark** bushes look down on the creek. Their clusters of white five-petaled flowers bloom in early summer. The shredded bark on this member of the rose family's older branches often identifies the bush. **Star Solomon seal** shows up in a thick colony of **wild geranium**. Watch for **giant rattlesnake plantain** on the upslope.

The trail drops back to the creek and makes another crossing. Rich red **crimson monkey flower** reflect in the pools starting to form in the creek. A few steps farther, the trail enters a meadow. Bursts of orange **western wallflower** around the meadow catch your attention. Tall **Hooker's evening primrose** line up near the trail with fresh yellow blossoms, and withered peach ones. **Mountain parsley** and **yarrow** spread across the field.

The creek draws closer to the trail, bringing with it **New Mexico raspberry** bushes dotted with big white flowers, and smaller **red raspberry** bushes. **Red cinquefoil, golden-beard penstemon,** and **skyrocket** color the path with their red blossoms. **Franciscan bluebell** and **verbena** add blue hues. Rusty relics of the sawmill appear with the florals in the field.

At about mile 1.7, a horse path on the left detours equestrians around a section of slickrock. **Red-osier dogwood** encroaches as the trail squeezes between silvery slickrock formations and the creek. You can see why the flexible dogwood branches were used in basketmaking as you bend them back to pass along the trail. Basketry is the more aesthetic use of the bush, dogwood got its name from a species in England used to wash mangy dogs.

After a dicey scramble across the creek, the trail clings to the east wall where **alumroot** carpets shady slopes. Just before the trail makes its final creekcrossing for this hike, it peers down a steep sheet of slickrock where Ash Creek Falls starts its 200-foot descent. You can view the falls from a rocky vantage point at mile 2.5, just beyond where the horse detour joins the trail. Return the way you came.

RED CINQUEFOIL
Potentilla thurberi

Potentilla comes from the French, meaning "five fingers", another of red cinquefoil's common names. These five leaves sometimes get red cinquefoil and its cousins confused with strawberry before the plants bloom, not surprising, since both plants belong to the rose family. However, strawberry is a creeper and red cinquefoil stands upright.

The tannic acid in the leaves of some species of cinquefoil make them excellent astringents.

ASH CREEK TRAIL

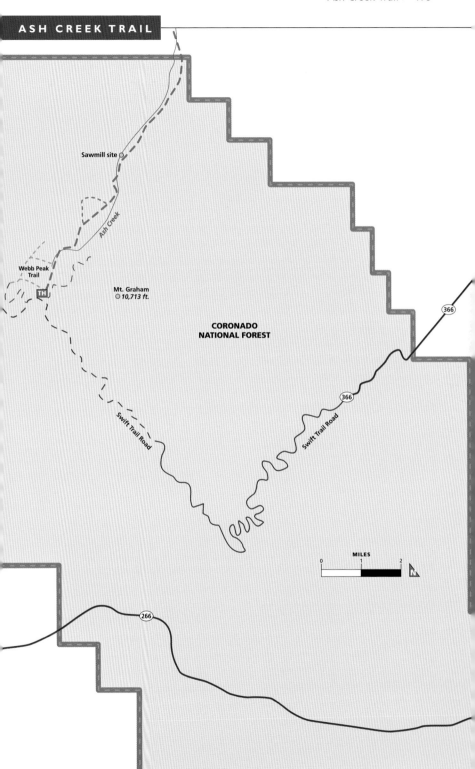

Sawmill site

Ash Creek

Webb Peak
Trail

TH

Mt. Graham
10,713 ft.

CORONADO
NATIONAL FOREST

366

366

Swift Trail Road

Swift Trail Road

MILES

0   1   2

N

266

Wildflower Hike 38

Upper Grant Creek

The short hike along upper Grant Creek rewards hikers with dozens of different wildflowers that color the creekbanks.

Trail Rating	Easy
Trail Length	0.2 mile one way
Location	Safford, Mount Graham
Elevation	9,000–9,050 feet
Contact	Coronado National Forest, Safford Ranger District, 928-428-4150
Bloom Season	July–September
Peak Bloom	August
Directions	From Safford, take US 191 south about 7 miles to AZ 366. Turn right (southwest) and drive about 7 miles (AZ 366 ends and becomes Swift Trail road). Continue another 16 miles on the winding Swift Trail road to an unsigned parking area on the north side of the road.

Grant Creek, a major drainage of the Pinaleno Mountains, tumbles with mountain water year round. The creek gets its name from Fort Grant, situated about 7 miles downstream. Fort Grant served as an outpost during the Apache conflicts from the time the government built the fort in 1872 to Geronimo's capture in 1886. With Fort Huachuca nearby, Fort Grant's importance gradually waned and it was finally abandoned in 1905.

The Grant Creek catchment becomes a melange of wildflowers when summer comes to the mountains. The constant supply of creekwater maintains the display of flowers, which spreads from the creekbanks across the nearby forest floor.

Richardson's geranium carpets the streamsides near the parking area, dotting the forest floor with its light pink blossoms. **Mouse-ear chickweed** blends in small white flowers with lobed petals. **Harebell** brings blue bell flowers to the spread and **wood sorrel** shows pink funnel flowers. The taller **nodding groundsel** and **yarrow** are easy to spot in this matted mix, but watch, too, for the shorter, distinctive-looking **verileaf phacelia** and **Scouler's catchfly.**

At the creek, the flowers line the banks like a colorful crowd watching the water parade downstream. **Crimson monkey flower** arbitrarily clusters along the banks. The stems of these flowers root at the nodes and grow in clumps around wet areas such as seeps in rocks or by streams. **Yellow columbine**, with its nectar-carrying spurs, arches over the water. **Willow weed** holds upright seedpods developed from its small pink clusters of flowers.

Yellow snapdragon-like blossoms of **common monkey flower** also gather in clumps along the banks at the feet of towering **cow parsnip** and **osha**. The large, elegant fern growing from the banks is **lady fern.**

CREEPING BARBERRY
Berberis repens

In another century, you might have picked a spray of barberry to keep witches away from you. Today, you're much better off leaving their creeping stems intact and enjoying the clusters of yellow flowers that bloom on the plant in the springtime.

Look for creeping barberry to appear most often in pine forests, but you'll also find them in subalpine biomes.

The purple berries of the foot-long plants make a drink akin to lemonade. The Navajo use an infusion of its twigs and leaves for rheumatism.

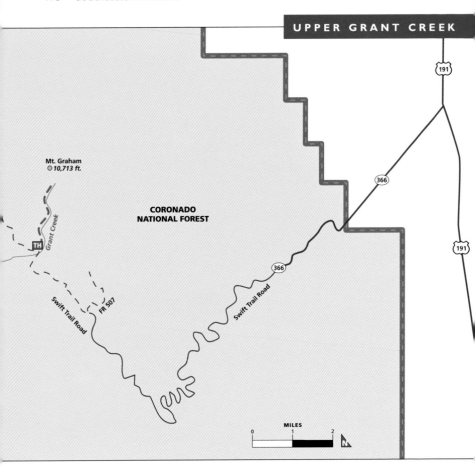

Mt. Graham
◎ 10,713 ft.

CORONADO
NATIONAL FOREST

Grant Creek

TH

Swift Trail Road

FR 507

Swift Trail Road

366

366

191

191

MILES
0   1   2

N

Cleavers spray tiny white flowers from velcro-like leaves and stems that tangle in logs and limbs in the creekbed. You may see **large-flowered brickellbush** climbing the rocky slope overlooking the west bank.

Looking upstream, head for a cascade spilling over a tree trunk to follow along the creek. Check for **polemonium** and **Franciscan bluebell** dangling over the water. From here, you can follow a footpath that develops from the parking area and parallels the stream.

Palm-sized **thimbleberry** leaves gather along the path and spill down the drainage slope to the creek. You may see the plant's raspberry-like fruit if the animals haven't plucked it first. Bunches of **wild strawberry** mix with **Richardson's geranium** and **mountain parsley** at a primitive camp spot.

As the trail veers toward the creek, dainty-leaved **meadow rue** rubs shoulders with **New Mexico locust**. **Meadow rue** often has small tassel flowers hanging from its branches throughout the summer while **New Mexico locust** displays its flowers only in early summer. The seeds, bark, and roots of the locust are poisonous to humans, but the mauve-colored clusters of pea flowers are edible.

Staying close to the creek with **Richardson's geranium** in tow, the path passes **nodding groundsel** and **yellow columbine**. Be on the lookout, too, for **Canada violet**.

A short ancillary path leads to the drainage where **currant** bushes meet with alder trees. **Common monkey flower** and **scarlet monkey flower** color the creek. **Polemonium** stands tall next to **Franciscan bluebell**, which bows branches over a cascade of water splaying over a jumble of deadfall.

The next side-path to the creek, about 50 yards upstream, leads to an area that has the feel of a grotto with its cover of alder and maple trees and surrounding outcropping of rock. A moss-covered twist of tree roots from a dead, but still standing, giant fir attracts **yellow columbine** and **nodding groundsel**. **Baneberry** likes the creeksides.

As the footpath continues upstream, you may see **sweet Cicely** and **star Solomon's seal**. **Richardson's geranium** and **Canada violet** are always with you.

By about mile 0.2, the path becomes hard to follow because of jumbles of downfall. Return the way you came.

Wildflower Hike 39

Crest Trail

A large fire has created a good environment for wildflower growth along the Crest Trail.

In 1994, the Rattlesnake Fire burned 27,000 acres in the Chiricahua Mountains. Much of the Crest Trail shows charred scars from the burn, especially on the western slopes. Burn areas look unsightly, but often provoke wildflower growth, allowing more sun onto the forest floor, adding nutrients to the soil from the burned wood, and providing the disturbed ground so many wildflowers embrace.

The Crest Trail travels 10.3 miles along the Chiricahua's backbone. This route takes you 1.5 miles to Long Park, then loops back to the trailhead along a four-wheel-drive road that travels just down the eastern slope of the trail.

Trail Rating	Moderate
Trail Length	3-mile loop
Location	Chiricahua Mountains
Elevation	8,500–9,200 feet
Contact	Coronado National Forest, Douglas Ranger District, 520-364-3468
Bloom Season	July–early September
Peak Bloom	August
Special Considerations	The Forest Service charges a $3.00 user fee at the trailhead.
Directions	From Willcox, drive 23 miles southeast on AZ 186 and turn left (east) onto AZ 181. Drive 2.9 miles and turn right (south) onto Pinery Canyon Road/FR 42; drive 11.2 miles and turn right (south) onto FR 42D. Drive 2.7 miles to the trailhead.

The trail begins by switchbacking its way above the Rustler Park campground through colonies of **bracken fern** and **silver-stem lupine**. **Verbena**, **yellow evening primrose**, and **western dayflower** add color to the green cover.

The trail continues more steeply to a hilltop clearing spread with **silver-stem lupine** and **verbena**, then passes through a gate at about mile 0.2. Veer left for the Crest Trail.

Still climbing, the trail passes another clearing on the left where **larkspur** rises above **bracken fern**, and **sweet clover vetch** tangles among them. **Mexican silene** of the pink family edges the path, and **mountain spray** bushes stand back by the trees.

Watch for yellow and red **mountain parsley**, then **spreading four o'clock**. Stands of trees interrupt the long clearing along the trail as the path continues to climb. **Larkspur** prefers the sunny pockets, along with **Richardson's geranium** and **Fendler's potato**. **Wood sorrel** and **bracted strawberry** show up in the shade alongside the trail.

At about mile 0.5, a burn area looks messy with downfall and scorched tree skeletons, but the trailsides fill with **Richardson's geranium, currant** bushes, and **mullein**. Hummingbirds sip from **golden-beard penstemon**. The charred devastation, colored with wildflowers, makes a strangely beautiful sight. The trail leaves the burn area and passes through a shady stretch where **Canada violet** and **Richardson's geranium** cover the forest floor.

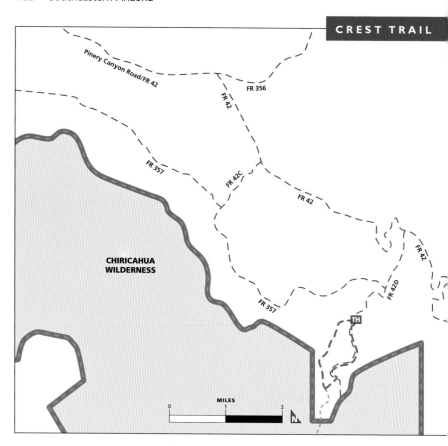

The next burn area is brushy with **red raspberry** bushes chafing against the path. **New Mexico locust** shows bold thorns. Boughs of **blue elderberry** drip grape-colored berries into the path. A colony of **mullein** appears just down the trail.

At about mile 0.6, a **bracted strawberry** patch nestles in a pocket on the west side of the trail. Just across from the berry patch, look for **pine trumpet.** **Giant hyssop** displays rose-pink clusters of flowers separated down its stem. A seep oozing from a rock wall ahead drains along the trail here and creates a nice moist area that attracts **alumroot** and **red raspberry.**

At the rock wall, about mile 0.7, red, orange, and yellow **columbine** climb around the craggy rock. **Alumroot** dusts the gray wall with its tiny, light-pink flower clusters. **Golden draba** climbs with **large-flowered brickellbush, wood sorrel,** and **Cockerell's sedum. Many-flowered stick seed** tangles with **groundsel** along one side of the trail, and **Richardson's geranium** on the other.

The trail leaves this moist environment and finds flowers that can tolerate a drier atmosphere, such as **yarrow, Indian paintbrush, verbena,** and **western**

dayflower. A panorama to the east glances into New Mexico, past the jagged ridgelines of the Chiricahua Mountains.

Gambel oak trees follow the path of a seep down a sunny bedrock slope at about mile 1. A collection of color pools around the trail: deep red **Lemmon's sage**, rose-purple **spreading four o'clock**, **Thurber's gilia** (which looks like its cousin **skyrocket**, but purple), and electric-purple **verbena**. These flowers reappear in another meadow at about mile 1.1. Look for **verileaf phacelia**, too.

The trail ducks into the forest again, passing Hillside Spring, and then continues in filtered light that causes the trail to lose touch with many of the wildflowers. But Long Park brings the botanicals back. The flower-filled field has a collection of **Rocky Mountain iris, sneezeweed**, and **larkspur**. Yellow-flowered **spur gentian** and **cow clover**, mottled pink and white, edge the trail. **Silver-stem lupine** and **golden-beard penstemon** hang around the outer perimeter of the meadow, near the rocky edge walling the west side of the field. If you take a moment to search the outcropping, you may see **fleabane, large-flowered brickellbush, mountain spray**, and **taperleaf** in the crevices.

You may follow the Crest Trail as long as you like, but to continue this hike, take the short footpath at the northeast end of the meadow that connects to FR 42D and head north toward the trailhead.

Most of the meadow flowers continue with the trail, filling in pockets of sunlight. Look for **nodding groundsel** and **mouse-ear chickweed** among the bunch. **Meadow rue** stays in the shade.

At about mile 1.6, the east roadside has an extraordinary display of **larkspur** flecked gold with **sneezeweed**. **Wood sorrel, cleavers**, and **Fendler's potato** grow like a groundcover around the tall flowers.

About 200 feet below the Crest Trail, the roadsides fill with sunlight and the trail-side flowers you saw earlier. At about mile 1.8, watch for a band of **American basketflower** about 20 feet above the road. This spiny thistle

AMERICAN BASKETFLOWER
Centaurea americana

The bold pink and white blossom of the American basketflower makes a stunning show along roadsides and in sunny meadows. Threadlike pink petals fringe a yellow center to make a blossom that can grow over 3 inches wide.

The *centaurea* genus has over 400 species. This cultivated species borders on noxious weed status.

has a delicate flurry of purple threadlike petals that surround the yellowish center of the flower.

A colony of **Thurber's gilia** fills the roadsides just before a bend. At the bend, look for **egg mat buckwheat, amber lily,** and **wild chrysanthemum** on the buff-colored bedrock on the upslope. **Sweet scent** has almost the same shade of purple blossoms as **Thurber's gilia**, but much smaller, and releases a sweet scent when crushed.

Mexican silene looks pretty on the next outcropping just down the hill. Across from it, **alumroot** grows upon a weeping rock. Colonies of **golden-beard penstemon, plains beebalm,** and **verbena** combine to create a colorful clearing at mile 2.25. **Golden-beard penstemon** heads downhill with the road into clusters of **Richardson's geranium** and **thermopsis. Yellow columbine** and **red raspberry** fill the moist roadsides along with **currant** bushes.

At about mile 2.6, the road drops down to Forest Service cabins, then edges Rustler Park and its spread of **sneezeweed** and wildflowers familiar to the trail. Continue on the roadway, back to the trailhead.

A large colony of larkspur gather along the Crest Trail.

Vault Mine Trail

*The Vault Mine Trail starts in Madera Canyon,
one of the world's top birding spots.*

Easy	**Trail Rating**
0.5 mile one way	**Trail Length**
Tucson, Mount Wrightson Wilderness	**Location**
5,240–5,390 feet	**Elevation**
Coronado National Forest, Nogales Ranger District, 520-281-2296	**Contact**
July–September	**Bloom Season**
August	**Peak Bloom**
This trail lies in the Mount Wrightson Wilderness Area, where no mechanized vehicles, including mountain bikes, are allowed. The Forest Service suggests a $3.00 donation to enter the wilderness.	**Special Considerations**
From Tucson, take I-19 south to Continental Road (Exit 63); go left and drive about 9 miles southeast (the road becomes Continental-White House Canyon Road/FR 62). When you get to Madera Canyon Road (FR 70), turn right (south) and drive about 5 miles to the Old Baldy/Vault Mine Trailhead.	**Directions**

After the Planchas de Plata silver strike in 1736, waves of miners headed to the Santa Rita Mountains to plumb precious minerals from the mountains' golden granite depths. First came the Spanish, then the Jesuits via Indian workmen. The Apache Indians, however, forced them out.

In the mid-1850s, a handful of savvy Anglo prospectors tried to reopen the abandoned mines. But the Apache Indians cleared them out, too.

With Indian wars and mining the mountain passé, the lovely mountain range has recouped its peaceful demeanor. Now natural features and wildlife, rather than precious metals and bloodshed, draw attention to the mountains.

One of the Santa Rita Mountains' more idyllic spots, Madera Canyon, has become one of the top birding areas in the world. About 240 species of birds live in the canyon. The Vault Mine Trail gets its start in Madera Canyon.

The first half mile of the Vault Mine Trail follows a drainage that draws a variety of wildflowers. This hike ends when the trail pulls away from the drainage at a waterfall that cascades down a slot of rocks.

BOUVARDIA
Bouvardia glaberrima

The bouvardia bush, with its appealing red trumpet-shaped flowers, fits its Spanish name *trompetilla,* or "little trumpet." Bouvardia, like most red tube flowers, is designed to accommodate hummingbirds. Insects don't see the color red, but hummingbirds do. Also, hummingbirds can reach down into the well of the tube to sip the flowers' pools of nectar.

The hike starts out in a sunny and dry section that parallels a picnic area in Madera Canyon. **Plains beebalm** and **wild chrysanthemum** line up along the trailsides.

At about mile 0.1, look for **coral bells** lodged in a cross-drainage that drops down the eastern upslope, across the trail, and continues down to the drainage on the west. The coral-colored clusters show up vividly with the more demure **sweet scent.**

Fleabane and **pink windmill** swagger along the trailsides, and **narrow-leaf tick clover** crawls around them as the path continues toward the Old Baldy Trail. A field at about mile 0.25 fills with spikes of white- and purple-clustered **plains beebalm.** Watch for **Texas betony** at the intersection with the Old Baldy Trail.

Just beyond the Old Baldy Trail, the path comes to a clearing filled with flowers. **Texas betony's** deep red elongated clusters draw attention, then the vibrant purples of **wild geranium** and **verbena** come into view. **Plains beebalm** prevails in the sunny spaces. You can tell **Texas betony** and **plains beebalm** belong to the mint family because they have square stems.

As you study the meadow a little longer, you may find **western dayflower, white nightshade, scarlet gaura**, and **amber lily**. **Field mint** and **sweet scent**, two more mint family members, tend toward the areas shaded by Arizona sycamore trees, along with **red figwort** and **cleavers**. **Poison ivy** and snakes like the shade, too. Be careful when picking around near the trees.

Plains beebalm follows you out of the field, and back onto the trail, which narrows to a ledge and peers into the drainage. **Hooker's evening primrose** grows on the upslope with **fleabane**. When the path widens again, watch for **nodding onion** and **bouvardia**.

The path takes a more rugged demeanor as it climbs up sections of jagged bedrock above the stream. **Pink windmill**, clusters of **verbena**, and groups of **western dayflower** follow along. **Hill's lupine**, already flowered but still recognizable by its downy palmate leaves, signals the trail is near the destination cascade that gushes from moss-lined slabs of rock. **Yellow columbine** gives the drainage a rock garden appeal as it hangs on the chasm's deep walls. Return the way you came.

WILD GERANIUM
Geranium caespitosum

Whenever a hike travels into a pine forest, wild geranium is usually close by. The deep pink flowers remain faithful to the trailsides even when the trail pulls away from a water source.

This member of the geranium family also goes by the name cranesbill. This name comes from the shape of its seedpod. Another name, *patita de leon,* comes from its leaf, which looks like a lion's paw.

Its cousin, Richardson's geranium, likes higher elevations and more moisture. You often find it in mixed conifer forests. It has pale blossoms, ranging from white to pale pink or purple, with purple veins.

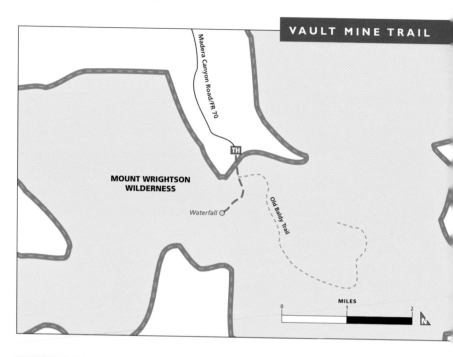

VAULT MINE TRAIL

Madera Canyon Road/FR 70

TH

MOUNT WRIGHTSON
WILDERNESS

Waterfall ○

Old Baldy Trail

MILES
0   1   2

N

*Wildflowers can be found
tucked away in various
rocky nooks and crannies
along the Vault Mine Trail.*

Marshall Gulch Trail

Yellow columbine is just one of many wildflowers that grow alongside the Marshall Gulch Trail.

Easy	**Trail Rating**
1.2 miles	**Trail Length**
Tucson, Mount Lemmon	**Location**
7,360–8,115 feet	**Elevation**
Coronado National Forest, Santa Catalina Ranger District, 520-749-8700	**Contact**
May–August	**Bloom Season**
August	**Peak Bloom**
The Forest Service charges a $5 fee for recreational use of Mount Lemmon.	**Special Considerations**
From I-10 in Tucson, drive east on Grant Road to Tanque Verde Road and continue east to the Catalina Highway. Turn left (northeast) and drive 25 miles up the mountain, through the town of Summerhaven, and go left (south) on FR 10 about 1.5 miles to the trailhead.	**Directions**

Treading through a forested canyon that holds moisture even during the driest months, the Marshall Gulch Trail has a particularly rich array of ferns, wildflowers, berry bushes, and giant firs and pines. The forest has a gothic look, with moss-topped giant gray boulders and a tangle of tree roots crossing the trail to draw moisture from the perennial creek.

Before you reach the trailhead, take a look at an island next to the parking area that may have a colony of **cosmos** blooming light-purple daisies. Across the road, **red figwort** and **silver-stem lupine** mix in with **ageratina** along the drainage. **Poison ivy**, which prefers to grow in disturbed places, hangs right around the trailhead sign and is seen often along the trail. Be careful of this irritating plant.

GREEN-FLOWERED MACROMERIA

Macromeria viridiflora

Like most of its cousins in the borage family, the yard-high green-flowered macromeria is covered with bristly hairs. Even the long, greenish trumpet flowers have a cover of hair.

The hairs, highly flammable when dried, make the plant an excellent addition to a smoking mixture. The Hopi Indians dried the green-flowered macromeria's leaves and flowers and mixed them with wild tobacco to use in rainmaking ceremonies.

Look for green-flowered macromeria in moist areas in conifer forests, especially near streambanks or edging clearings.

As you enter the woodland right next to the drainage, you may spot over a dozen different wildflowers within the first 100 yards. If it's early in the season, white umbels on tall **cow parsnip** plants lining the banks of the creek may catch your eye. Named *Heracleum lanatum* for the over-sized mythical character Hercules, the biggest member of the parsley family lives up to its name. Closer to the water, elegant **yellow columbine** arches over clumps of **crimson monkey flower**. **Cleavers** spray their tiny white blossoms among the mossy, streamside rocks.

Large-flowered brickell-bush and **wild geranium** squeeze in among **red-osier dogwood** bushes that overflow from the streambed onto the trailside. Clusters of **mountain parsley** fleck the other side of the trail with yellow, and **Canada violet** dots it white.

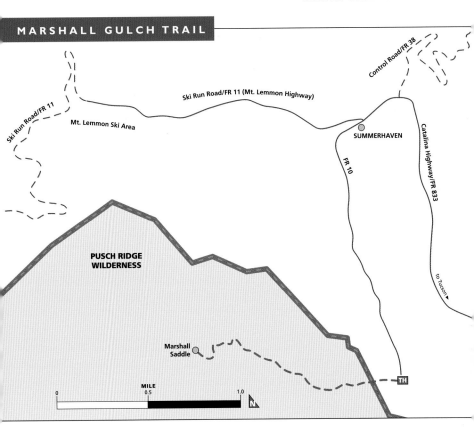

A bit farther, **false Solomon's seal** sprouts white berries that will eventually turn red-purple, and **baneberry** shows gleaming red berries. **Green-flowered macromeria** and **ageratina** fill the upslope.

The trail follows the gulch, crossing the stream often. **Agrimonia** crowds around streamcrossings, and **brown-eyed Susan** is usually nearby. Like its cousin, **Arizona rose, agrimonia** likes to grow around streams. Without the flowers (dime-sized yellow on the **agrimonia**, and inch-wide pink on **Arizona rose**), the two look alike at first glance. However, **agrimonia** has hairy stems, and thorns grow on the **Arizona rose's** stems.

You may spot **field mint** and **heal all** right along the streambanks. Both of these flowers belong to the mint family. In the small grassy clearings running up from the gulch, **Indian paintbrush, ageratina,** and **Arizona cudweed** fill in the dapples of sun.

Deep in the gulch, where pewter-gray walls drip with seeps and thick mats of moss cover giant boulders, the trail takes on temperate rainforest characteristics. **Red-osier dogwood** forms thickets in the gulch. **Alumroot** likes to hang out on the weeping rock walls.

At about mile 0.6, the trail brushes past **crimson monkey flower** nestled against a stone wall covered with moss, ferns, **wood sorrel**, and **bracted strawberry**. Look for **Cockerell's sedum** on the rock wall's narrow ledges.

As the trail gains in elevation, watch for **mountain ash** trees displaying orange clusters of berries. Not a true ash, which belongs to the olive family, this mountain ash comes from the rose family. Its white clusters of flowers bloom in June.

By about mile 1, the trail climbs away from the stream. Though the flowers thin out, you may still see **yarrow, New Mexico locust**, and occasional **wild geranium**. The trail ends at the intersections with several other trails at Marshall Saddle. Return the way you came.

The Marshall Gulch Trail brushes past a moss-covered rock wall full of bracted strawberry and wood sorrel.

Upper Sabino Canyon Riparian Area

Yellow columbine arch into the trail in the Upper Sabino Canyon Riparian Area.

The lower reaches of Sabino Canyon, with its developed trail system, shuttle cars, and visitor center, grab most of the attention for this major drainage system of the Santa Catalina Mountains. The opposite of the wide-open desert terrain of lower Sabino Canyon, the upper end, where the canyon gets its start at the top of Mount Lemmon, has a narrow corridor cloistered by trees and is packed with botanicals.

From the Mount Lemmon Ski Area, the trail makes a sunny descent into the canyon past rose-purple flowers on **wild geranium**, tall **Hooker's evening primrose** displaying fresh yellow blossoms and spent

Trail Rating	Easy
Trail Length	1.0 mile
Location	Tucson, Mount Lemmon
Elevation	8,000–8,300 feet
Contact	Coronado National Forest, Santa Catalina Ranger District, 520-749-8700
Bloom Season	July–September
Peak Bloom	August
Special Considerations	The Forest Service charges a $5 fee for recreational use of Mount Lemmon.
Directions	From I-10 in Tucson, drive east on Grant Road to Tanque Verde Road and continue east to the Catalina Highway. Turn left (northeast) and drive up the mountain to Ski Run Road/FR 11 (Mt. Lemmon Highway, just before Summerhaven). Turn right (west) and follow the road to the Mount Lemmon Ski Area and park. Cross the road to the guardrail across from the Iron Door Restaurant, and follow the path to the Upper Sabino Canyon Riparian Area.

orange flowers, and **goldenrod**. The ski lift to the country's southernmost ski area strings up a slope to the west. **Sweet clover vetch** twines in the tall grasses along the path. **Fleabane** displays clusters of white daisies, and **cleavers** climb in rocks along the trail.

Red raspberry bushes begin edging the path when it reaches a mixed conifer forest. **Golden-beard penstemon** and **red figwort** head for sunny clearings. By mile 0.1, **yellow columbine** and **Richardson's geranium** appear in the canyon. These wildflowers appear almost constantly throughout the trail. Follow the path past a fence. At a fork in the trail, about mile 0.2, veer left.

Canada violet joins the columbine-geranium cover. Its white flowers and branched leaf system differentiate this violet from others. You can recognize the parsley family's **cow parsnip** in the streambed right away by its massive, many-pointed leaves.

At about mile 0.3, the trail passes a sign identifying the Upper Sabino Canyon Riparian Area. Just beyond, a streamside clearing makes room for **red figwort** and **nodding groundsel**. The upslope has a green carpet of foliage dotted yellow and mauve from the constant cover of **yellow columbine** and **Richardson's geranium**. **Mountain parsley** shows up at a fork in the trail, where you veer right.

The trail squeezes through a meeting of **nodding groundsel, agrimonia,** and **yellow columbine**. Though its tiny yellow elongated clusters of flowers differ from its cousin rose, **agrimonia** has a similar leaf system. This can cause confusion differentiating between the two before they flower.

The trail enters a moist area where seeps ooze from the aspen-covered upslope into the stream running alongside the trail below. Lichens mottle the forest floor and drip from conifer branches. **False Solomon's seal** cascades from the upslope. You may see white or purple berries clustered at its tip. The berries are edible, but tend to be bitter. The clusters of red berries on **baneberry** bushes have an attractive appeal, too. But stay away, because these berries are very poisonous, and interfere with heart function.

Scarlet monkey flower clambers up a feeder drainage about 100 feet farther on the trail. Moisture-loving **Curly dock** hangs around a spring that gently flows over the path.

A very pretty mixture of **mountain parsley, fleabane, nodding groundsel, Richardson's geranium, brown-eyed Susan,** and **Indian paintbrush** spreads around the trailsides as the trail drops to join a road near mile 0.7. Watch for a particularly attractive section of the stream below, just past two large tanks. **Cow parsnip** fills a bench while **Hooker's evening primrose** and **mullein** stand in the background. **Scarlet monkey flower** dots

YELLOW COLUMBINE
Aquilegia chrysantha

Yellow columbine gravitates to water, and you can find it growing on the banks of mountain streams, hanging on weeping canyon walls, or gathered in moist areas of shady forests. The complicated blossom of the flower looks, at first blush, like five petals. When you consider the blossom from the side, you can see that each petal elongates into a spur. Its scientific name, *Aquilegia,* probably stems from the Latin word *aquilegus,* or "water container," for each of these spurs contains a pool of nectar for pollinators to sip from.

Not every pollinator that approaches the yellow columbine gets to drink the nectar. Only the hawkmoth has a tongue long enough to lap the liquid. The moth brushes up against the flower's pollen as it hovers and sips.

Hummingbirds pollinate the red columbine, which has shorter spurs.

The lovely columbine has intriguing esoteric meanings. The flower, because of its hornlike spurs, represents disloyalty. On the other hand, the flower also represents doves (columbine derives from the Latin *columba,* or dove). It often appears in religious paintings symbolizing the dove of peace, or the Holy Spirit.

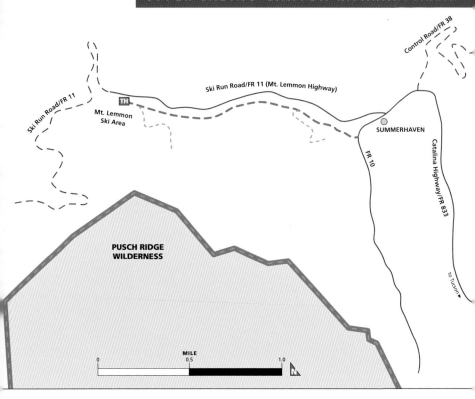

the streambed red and **willow weed** shows small pink flowers. **Brown-eyed Susan** provides feeding pads for butterflies.

At about mile 0.7, the creek flows under the road through a culvert. If you follow a beaten path a few steps away to the stream, now on the west side of the trail, you may see orange **daylily** line the stream with **agrimonia.**

The Upper Sabino Canyon Riparian Area ends at a small parking area ringed by **agrimonia** and **red raspberry**, near a sign identifying the area. Return the way you came.

Butterfly Trail

This trail passes through different environments such as meadows and riparian areas. Each has a unique collection of wildflowers.

Strenuous	**Trail Rating**
2.7–5.2 miles one way	**Trail Length**
Tucson	**Location**
6,700–8,400 feet	**Elevation**
Coronado National Forest, Santa Catalina Ranger District, 520-749-8700	**Contact**
July–early September	**Bloom Season**
August	**Peak Bloom**
The Forest Service charges a $5 recreation user fee on Mount Lemmon.	**Special Considerations**
From I-10 in Tucson, drive east on Grant Road to Tanque Verde Road and continue east to the Catalina Highway. Turn left (northeast) and drive past milepost 21 to FR 2, the first turnoff to Mt. Bigelow. Turn right and go 0.1 mile to FR 34 and turn right (east). Drive 1.2 miles to the parking area at the end of the road.	**Directions**

The Butterfly Trail probably got its name when the trail's designer, Fred Kimball, commented on the numerous butterflies in the area. At the time, the trail had more open fields with old-growth pines. These open parklike stands of pines allowed thousands more flowers, which attract butterflies.

With an elevation span of 1,700 feet, and environments ranging from oak communities to moist canyons, the Butterfly Trail hosts a large variety of botanicals. This section experiences the most abundant displays of wildflowers along the trail.

BANEBERRY
Actaea rubra

Unless you see baneberry in the early summer, you probably won't see their clusters of small white flowers blooming from their toothed leaves. An occasional late bloomer will display its flowers in August, but most baneberry bushes display their red berries by then.

The red berries immediately stand out in the surrounding green foliage. In their beginning stages, the berries are white and look like glistening china. This gives the bush its alternate name of chinaberry. The pretty berries are poisonous, however.

The trail starts on a sunny hillside across from the Mount Bigelow Lookout Tower. **Golden-beard penstemon** and **red figwort** lead to a cluster of **mountain spray** bushes. The pink buds on **mountain spray** give a pink tinge to its white clusters of flowers. You may see **ageratina** lined up to the left of the path. **Ageratina** has white, rayless flower clusters and heart-shaped, toothed leaves.

As the trail heads into the hillside clearing, **Scouler's catchfly, mountain parsley,** and **aspen fleabane** intersperse in colonies of **western dayflower** and **cosmos.** At the turn of a bend, the trail leaves the full sun and starts its long descent to Novio Spring under the cover of a mixed conifer forest. **Sweet clover vetch, mountain parsley,** and **wild geranium** crowd around the trail just before it drops into the shadowy depths of the forest.

Yellow columbine and **meadow rue** feel at home on the damp slopes and flourish in folds as the trail zigzags steeply. **Star Solomon seal** likes to gather near shady spots under large fir trees with **wood sorrel. Red figwort**

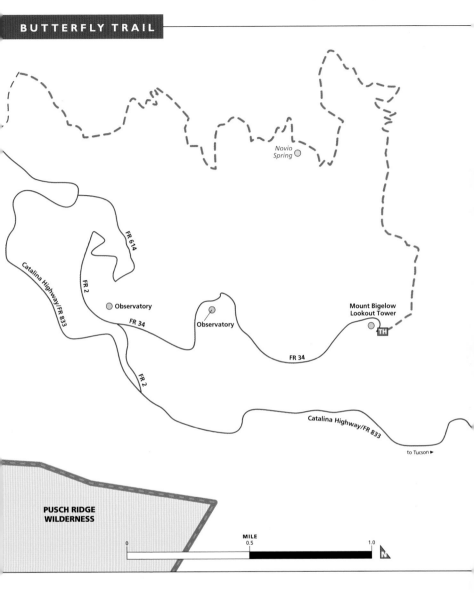

and **golden-beard penstemon** tend toward sunny dapples. **Baneberry, verileaf phacelia,** and **Canada violet** line the path in filtered light.

In rare sun-drenched clearings, **large-flowered brickellbush** and **Fendler's potato** join clusters of **western dayflower** and **aspen fleabane.** One particular clearing, at about mile 1, presents a stunning panorama to the east. You may see **New Mexico checkermallow** and a colony of **cosmos** following a natural drainage down the hillside. **Alumroot** and **spreading four o'clock** wedge themselves in the slabs of rock along the trail.

The trail continues to edge the mountainside where the sun gets a chance to nurture **fleabane, amber lily, skyrocket, golden-beard penstemon,** and **Indian paintbrush. Sweet scent** lines segments of the path. If you crush a leaf of **sweet scent** in your fingers, it releases volatile oils that explain their common name. As soon as the trail heads back under the pines, watch for **red raspberry** and the reappearance of **alumroot.**

At about mile 1.7, **pink windmill** lines a large rock wall that rises from the ground. From here, the trail allows one more eastern panorama before it drops to Novio Spring. The trail enters another oak community just after passing the intersection with the Davis Springs Trail. The botanicals dwindle here in this drier environment to **mountain parsley, scruffy prairie clover,** and **star cloak fern.**

As you near Novio Spring, you can hear cascading water, and the environment turns richly verdant. **Virginia creeper** crawls along the path, mosses upholster boulders, and **wood sorrel** carpets the forest floor. **Yellow columbine** follows the drainage.

After the trail crosses the stream, it climbs above the drainage and watches the water rush toward a dramatic cascade. A narrow outcropping adjacent to the trail provides a vantage point to view the falls. Look for a vibrant colony of **Texas betony** just beyond the outcropping.

The outcropping makes a good turnaround point for a day hike. You may return the way you came, or continue another 2.5 miles to the trail's end.

Meadow Trail

A golden matrix of sneezeweed and sunflowers spread along the Meadow Trail.

The Meadow Trail provides an easy hike to a chain of clearings in a mixed conifer forest full of colorful blankets of wildflowers. The hike starts in the forest on a spur trail signed with a hiker icon. At a trail junction, mile 0.1, veer right onto the Meadow Trail.

The path turns from the forest out into its first meadow. You may spot **mountain parsley** among the blanket of **bracken fern** spreading along the southern trailside next to the forest. **Sneezeweed** and **sunflower**, with occasional coral patches from **Indian paintbrush**, cover the north side of the trail. Both of these yellow daisy flowers belong to the sunflower family. Look for white patches of **fleabane** and **Arizona cudweed**.

Trail Rating	Easy
Trail Length	0.5 mile one way
Location	Tucson, Mount Lemmon
Elevation	9,000–9,100 feet
Contact	Coronado National Forest, Santa Catalina Ranger District, 520-749-8700
Bloom Season	July–September
Peak Bloom	August
Special Considerations	The Forest Service charges a $5 fee for recreational use of Mount Lemmon.
Directions	From I-10 in Tucson, drive east on Grant Road to Tanque Verde Road. Continue east to the Catalina Highway. Turn left (northeast) and drive up the mountain. Turn right (west) onto Ski Run Road/FR 11 (Mt. Lemmon Highway), just before Summerhaven. Go past the Mount Lemmon Ski Area to its end at a parking area.

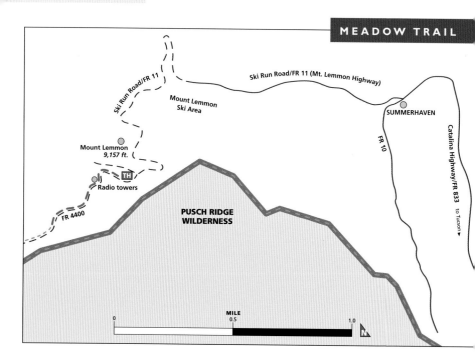

MEADOW TRAIL

The forest pulls back to allow room for the flowers to change sides along the trail. The flowers follow when the trail bends around the forest, kicking up a flurry of butterflies sipping from the **sneezeweed** and **sunflower**.

At about mile 0.3, the trail heads back into the pine forest. Most of the **sneezeweed** stays behind, but some, along with **fleabane**, **Richardson's geranium**, **Scouler's catchfly**, and **golden-beard penstemon**, show up in sunny dapples along the path.

When the trail steps into a meadow at about mile 0.4, a wave of yellow swirls around it from colonies of **sneezeweed** and **sunflower** that wend among the conifers like a golden matrix. **Richardson's geranium** creates pools tinged light purple. Watch for **wood sorrel**, **golden draba**, and **Fendler's potato** growing along a rotting log where the trail again re-enters the forest. **Sneezeweed** and **sunflower** beam from a pocket meadow beyond the trees.

A footpath just across the trail from the log will take you into a gorgeous meadow full of flowers. A blanket of **sneezeweed** and **sunflower** has threads of color from **mouse-ear chickweed**, **wood sorrel**, and **yarrow**.

The wildflowers dwindle dramatically as the trail makes its way down the mountainside through a pine forest toward the Mount Lemmon Trail. You may continue on the Meadow Trail another half mile to its end, or you may make this your turnaround point. Return the way you came.

SNEEZEWEED
Helenium hoopesii

Sneezeweed's reputation of making people sneeze provoked nurseries to change the plant's name to mountain daisy. Both names fit the distinctive daisy's nature. Preferring high elevations, sneezeweed often grows in colonies that spread across mountain clearings like an orange-yellow carpet. The pollen from these flowers can trigger allergic reactions in some people.

Besides its trademark long drooping petals, you can also identify the plant by its woolly leaves and stems. The roots have medicinal properties that help alleviate stomach distress.

Wildflower Hike 45 # Oracle Ridge Trail

Wildflowers gather on the sun-soaked high point of the Oracle Ridge Trail.

The Oracle Ridge Trail can take you from the mountaintops to the desert floor, but this hike stays in the cool high country of the Santa Catalina Mountains. The hike contours the slope of a peak, rises to the high point of the Oracle Ridge Trail, then returns to the trailhead.

Fendler's ceanothus bushes spread around the sunny clearing where the Oracle Ridge Trail starts. **Spreading four o'clock** and **wild geranium** run a trail of purple around **fleabane** and **ageratina**. **Golden-beard penstemon** dangle red tube flowers. Most of these flowers trickle along as the trail enters a pine-oak forest on the southwestern side of the mountain. **Aspen fleabane** makes a particularly big show, and **Indian paintbrush** and **Wright's deervetch** accumulate along the path.

Trail Rating	Easy
Trail Length	0.5 mile one way
Location	Tucson, Mount Lemmon
Elevation	7,800–7,960 feet
Contact	Coronado National Forest, Santa Catalina Ranger District, 520-749-8700
Bloom Season	July–September
Peak Bloom	August
Special Considerations	The Forest Service charges a $5 fee for recreational use of Mount Lemmon.
Directions	From I-10 in Tucson, drive east on Grant Road to Tanque Verde Road and continue east to the Catalina Highway. Turn left (northeast) and drive up the mountain to Control Road/FR 38. Turn right (north) and drive 0.3 mile to the signed trailhead.

ORACLE RIDGE TRAIL

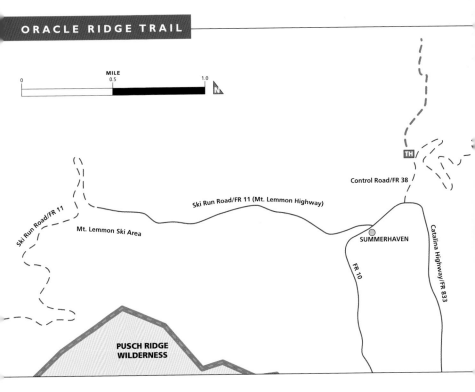

Stunning **coral bells** line up on a slabbed outcropping around mile 0.1. The elongated cluster of coral flowers top woolly stems. The round, scallop-edged leaves take the basal characteristics of its saxifrage family members. **Sweet scent** and **golden draba** like the rocky slab, too.

Look for **amber lily** on an outcropping on the other side of the trail. **Arizona cudweed, plains beebalm,** and Scouler's catchfly spread on the sunny downslope. Right along the path, **Hooker's evening primrose** displays its beautiful yellow night blooms, ready to wither to a soft orange color as the morning progresses. **Gray's lima bean** and **cleavers** crawl all around the slope.

The wildflower color is interrupted as the trail feels the shade of a handful of oaks. **Cleavers, Scouler's catchfly,** and **red figwort** become more noticeable. Then the path enters another sunny spot where **Fendler's ceanothus** and **wild chrysanthemum** flourish.

Back under the cover of oak trees, the trail curves around a rock wall where **sweet scent, cleavers,** and **golden draba** grow in clefts and niches; **red figwort** and **aspen fleabane** cover the wall. **Silver-stem lupine** appear when the trail steps into the sun. Check the downslope for the glow of **Indian paintbrush.** You also get glimpses of the Santa Catalina Mountains' precipitous cliffs in the distance through a filter of oak and mixed conifer trees.

At about mile 0.25, a drainage tumbles across the trail. On the upslope, a seep creates a mossy cover on a gray-colored outcropping. You may see **golden draba** hanging on the outcropping.

A few steps farther, the trail dries out in a sun-soaked clearing colored with **golden-beard penstemon, plains beebalm,** and **Thurber's gilia.** The purple flowers on **Thurber's gilia** are designed especially for hawkmoths to pollinate them. If you look closely, you can see the long thin tubes of the flowers bow slightly, causing the flower head to droop. Also, the petals on the flower turn back. These two features make the flowers off-limits to butterflies and bees because these

CORAL BELLS
Heuchera sanguinea

Coral bells make a pretty sight wherever they pop up—usually in a shaded cleft in a rock or on a canyon ledge. Their pleasant coral-red flowers cluster at the end of leafless stems rising from round basal leaves, and their roots have astringent properties.

pollinators need a perch to stand on when feeding. Hawkmoths, however, hover when they feed.

The trail rounds another bend to the northwest side of the peak. The oak trees stay behind, and the slope fills with mixed conifers. Their tan needles carpet the forest floor along with **wood sorrel, bracken fern,** and an occasional dot of wildflower color from **mountain parsley** and **wild geranium.**

The trail strings together a chain of island clearings that feature different wildflowers in each clearing. **Indian paintbrush** and **yarrow** collect in one, **Thurber's gilia** in another, and **plains beebalm** gathers with **western dayflower** and **wild parsley** in yet another.

At a clearing on the trail's high point, about mile 0.5, the trailsides gush with wildflowers. Almost all of the wildflowers seen so far on the trail meet here. Also look for **mouse-ear chickweed.** Return the way you came.

Indian paintbrush color a slope on the Oracle Ridge Trail.

*Wildflower
Hike 46*

Road to Mount Bigelow

*Wildflowers
grow on a slab
of rock along
the road to
Mount Bigelow.*

Mountain roadways, because of their propensity to become drainages during wet weather, often have excellent displays of wildflowers alongside as they wind through sunny sections on the mountains. The last 0.25 mile on the road to Mount Bigelow, a unique little section of the Santa Catalina Mountains, not only goes through a sunny berth on one of the mountains' peaks, but it also passes a seep under Palisade Rock that gathers an unusual blend of wildflowers.

A tall wall of **New Mexico raspberry** bushes lines the back of the parking area at the road's end. Their large white flowers develop into good-tasting red fruit similar to that of the familiar **red raspberry** you find later along the roadside.

Trail Rating	Easy
Trail Length	0.25 mile one way
Location	Tucson
Elevation	8,420–8,520 feet
Contact	Coronado National Forest, Santa Catalina Ranger District, 520-749-8700
Bloom Season	July–September
Peak Bloom	August
Special Considerations	The Forest Service charges a $5 recreational user fee on Mount Lemmon.
Directions	From I-10 in Tucson, drive east on Grant Road to Tanque Verde Road and continue east to the Catalina Highway. Turn left (northeast) and drive past milepost 21 to FR 2, the first turnoff to Mt. Bigelow. Turn right (north) and go 0.1 mile to FR 34 and turn right (east). Drive 1.2 miles to the parking area at the end of the road.

ROAD TO MOUNT BIGELOW

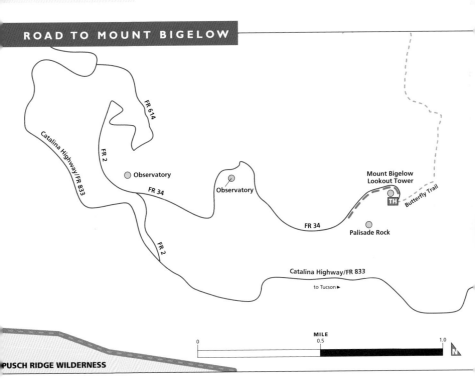

Jumbled in with the bushes, you may see bushy **red figwort** with its clusters of tiny red flowers and serrated arrow-shaped leaves. Also look for **Fendler's potato**, which looks like purple nightshade, **Scouler's catchfly**, and **cleavers**. **Golden-beard penstemon** displays its fabulous red tube flowers. **Indian paintbrush** and **yarrow** crowd around the sidewalk that leads up to the Mount Bigelow Lookout Tower.

Golden-beard penstemon and **red figwort** follow you to the road where you may see **ageratina**. Ageratina has white, rayless flower clusters and heart-shaped, toothed leaves. The leaves emit a pleasant fragrance when crushed. As the road bends west, a variety of bushes hug its edges: **mountain spray** has pink buds that open into white clusters, **red raspberry** bushes show ripe red berries, more **New Mexico raspberry** bushes show up, and towering **blue elderberry** has purple clusters of berries.

COCKERELL'S SEDUM
Sedum cockerellii

The orpine family members often have succulent features. Fleshy leaves and stems with a waxy coating protect the plants from moisture loss. The succulent Cockerell's sedum has this protective quality. Often growing in shady locations in rocky areas, the plant splays a half foot across ledges, mossy boulders, or rock-ribbed sections of forest ground. Pale pink star flowers top leaf-covered stems.

A steep rock wall pushes through the upslope on the south side of the road at about mile 0.1 where plants gather in hanging-garden fashion. A seep in the bedrock creates a favorable environment for moisture-loving plants.

Dainty pink flowers dangle from foot-long stems of **alum-root**. The root of this plant has astringent properties. **Wood sorrel** walks across narrow, moss-covered ledges. Rosette-shaped leaves from **saxifrage** plants that bloomed earlier in the spring squeeze in cracks. **Cockerell's sedum** clusters on flat slabs of rock. **Golden draba** climbs the rock, but also mixes with **Richardson's geranium** flowers that fill the roadside, where **meadow rue** displays tasseled blossoms.

Many of these flowers have characteristics that help retain

moisture. **Alumroot** and **golden draba** have thick covers of hair, and **Cockerell's sedum** and **saxifrage** are succulents. This helps them conserve water on this sun-drenched rock wall. **Meadow rue** and **Richardson's geranium** on the roadside are nurtured by pools of precipitation pouring from the rock wall and streaming down the roadside.

Red raspberry bushes line up on the other side of the road, sometimes with **blue elderberry** watching over them, and often with **plains beebalm** and **golden-beard penstemon** pushing in between them. A sunny slope filled with **plains beebalm** at mile 0.25 ends this walk. Return the way you came.

Cockerell's sedum

*Wildflower
Hike 47*

Comfort Spring Trail

Lemmon's sage colors to a rocky ledge along the Comfort Spring Trail.

Trail Rating	Moderate
Trail Length	1 mile one way
Location	Sierra Vista
Elevation	6,700–7,450 feet
Contact	Coronado National Forest, Sierra Vista Ranger District, 520-378-0311
Bloom Season	July–early September
Peak Bloom	August
Special Considerations	The road may be rocky and rutted; high-clearance vehicles are recommended.
Directions	From Sierra Vista, drive 2.5 miles east on AZ 90 and turn right (south) on AZ 92. Drive to Carr Canyon Road (FR 368), and turn right (west); follow the road 7.75 miles to the trailhead located just inside the Ramsey Vista Campground.

Comfort Spring got its name from a logging camp built nearby in the early 1900s, named Camp Comfort. Most of the remnants of the camp were burned in a 1977 fire, including a haunted cabin.

During a severe winter in the early 1930s, several woodcutters died of pneumonia. Their spirits supposedly haunted the cabin. The cabin's incineration in the 1977 fire, however, remedied any further ghost stories.

Bordered by **point leaf manzanita** bushes, the trail starts on the downhill heading into Carr Canyon. Wildflowers appear as the trail drops—slowly, at first, starting with **fleabane** and **ageratina**. Then **Mexican silene** colors the trailsides. **Sweet scent**, which produces a pleasant aroma when crushed in your fingers, also appears.

At a particularly scenic overlook into Carr Canyon, the surrounding forested slopes and peaks dip and swell like a restless sea. Rocky outcroppings bulge out into the trail. Across the canyon, the walls show off stacked spires and crimped outcroppings colored chartreuse from lichen.

At the first trailside outcropping, **star cloak fern** nestle in its ledges, and colonies of **Lemmon's sage** and **amber lily** color its top. A few steps farther, watch for the red tubes of **bouvardia** just before **cosmos** lines the trail. Where the **cosmos** ends, **Hooker's evening primrose** takes over.

When the trail descends into a drainage, **Gray's lima bean** drapes down the slopes and **canyon grape** twines around trees. **Wild geranium** edges the trail, and **American basketflower** congregates in the middle of the drainage. Just after the drainage **yellow daisy**, and **red raspberry** crowd around the trail. A bit farther, watch for colonies of **larkspur** on the left and **verbena** on the right. Then continue to watch for **poison ivy**, which proliferates on either side of the trail.

Indian paintbrush beams near **large-flowered brickellbush** as the trail climbs out of the drainage and into another. The trail passes a colony of **creeping barberry**, ripe with blue berries, just before reaching Comfort Spring, a square concrete trough with a flow of water (purify it before you drink it). At Comfort Spring, return the way you came.

LARKSPUR
Delphinium sp.

Larkspur like to gather in moist forest clearings or meadows. The deep blue coloration of the flowers creates a striking scene.

Larkspur has a masterfully designed pollination scheme well-suited for bumblebees. These bees must push aside the flower petals and wrangle through the stamens to get to the cache of nectar pooled in its backward spur.

The plant also has a powerful self-defense system against livestock and herbivores. It contains toxic alkaloids and delphinine, which makes it one of the more poisonous plants in the mountains.

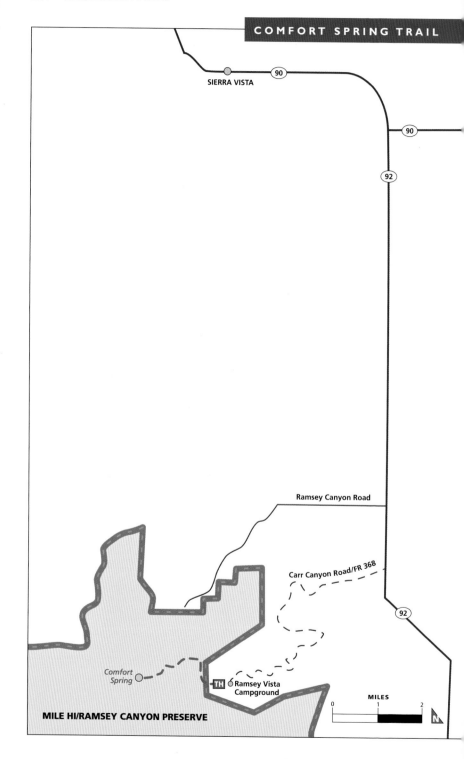

Carr Peak Trail

Two forest fires have created prime conditions for wildflower growth on the Carr Peak Trail.

Strenuous	**Trail Rating**
4.4 miles one way	**Trail Length**
Sierra Vista	**Location**
7,225–9,446 feet	**Elevation**
Coronado National Forest, Sierra Vista Ranger District, 520-378-0311	**Contact**
July–September	**Bloom Season**
August	**Peak Bloom**
The road may be rocky and rutted; high-clearance vehicles are recommended.	**Special Considerations**
From Sierra Vista, drive 2.5 miles east on AZ 90 and turn right (south) on AZ 92. Drive to Carr Canyon Road (FR 368), and turn right (west); follow the road 7.5 miles to the trailhead located at road's end just outside of the Ramsey Vista Campground.	**Directions**

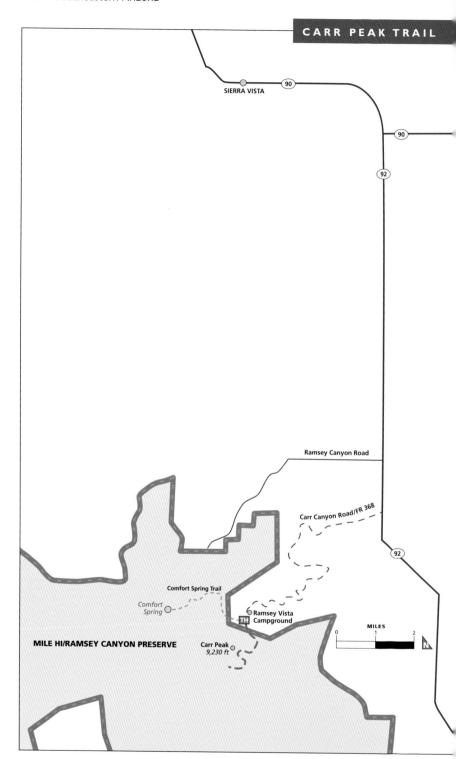

CARR PEAK TRAIL

SIERRA VISTA
90
90
92

Ramsey Canyon Road

Carr Canyon Road/FR 368

92

Comfort Spring Trail

*Comfort
Spring*

Ramsey Vista
TH Campground

MILE HI/RAMSEY CANYON PRESERVE

Carr Peak
9,230 ft

MILES
0   1   2

N

Thanks to two fires in 1977 and 1991, which opened up the mountaintop to sunshine and nutrients, the Carr Peak Trail generally produces an extraordinary show of wildflowers each year. Also, the trail sits at an intersection of several different vegetation influences, and this greatly increases the variety of wildflowers.

In the beginning of its continuous climb up to Carr Peak, the trail passes **Thurber's gilia** and **amber lily** in small clearings wedged in a hedge of **point leaf manzanita** bushes cloistering the trail.

Right after passing the intersection with the Comfort Spring Trail (see p. 210), views of the San Pedro Valley open up to the east. The city of Sierra Vista splays across the valley. The Mule and Dragoon mountains rise behind the city in the east.

When the trail levels off momentarily, **fleabane, Wright's deervetch, Arizona cudweed,** and **western dayflower** scatter around a rocky clearing. A stand of ponderosa pines signals you to watch for a drainage full of flowers on the right. If you take a moment to peruse the shallow drainage, you may see **pleated gentian, golden-beard penstemon, Indian paintbrush, goldenrod,** and a species of yellow daisy that some botanists call DYC, meaning "damn yellow composites." With so many species of yellow daisylike flowers in the sunflower (*Compositae*) family, DYC is the catch-all term when an expert isn't around to delineate any fine-line discrepancies between the species.

Just past the pines, **wild geranium** and **ageratina** crowd around the trail and blanket the mountainslopes. Also look for **plains bee balm** and **white sweet clover** among the mix. Blankets of **yellow daisy** gather at the wilderness boundary, then colonies of **cosmos** join the colorful show. Also watch for **nodding onion.**

ERYNGO
Eryngium heterophyllum

This parsley family member will make you look twice if you come across its flower. Eryngo, or coyote thistle, looks like a leftover shell of a flower with its unusual inflorescence. Real petals do exist on the plant, on the cluster of minuscule blue flowers in the center of a circle of stiff, prickly bracts. You might find eryngo along roadsides or trail gullies.

As the trail continues its climb, colonies of **sweet scent** appear with **Thurber's gilia**. At about mile 1.5, after the trail ducks into a mix of conifers, **yellow daisy** covers a clearing with bursts of electric-purple **verbena**.

The trail pushes through a thicket of **snowberry** and **New Mexico locust** bushes, then crosses a slab of bedrock. Just beyond the bedrock, look for **green gentian, western blue flax** and **New Mexico raspberry**. Also look for the unusual **eryngo**. The member of the parsley family looks nothing like its relatives, but more like a leftover shell of a flower.

Since the 1977 fire cleared the upper reaches of the mountain, a young stand of aspens has taken hold on the slopes of the peak. **Yellow columbine, cleavers, osha, pine trumpet,** and **red raspberry** feel comfortable in the aspen forest's moist environment.

The trail gets a brief break from the shade when it enters a meadow full of **cosmos** before heading back into the aspens. Once above the aspens, however, ridgetop meadows become a riot of color with **yellow daisy, wild geranium, Lemmon's sage,** and **plains bee balm**.

Then at mile 4.1 the spur trail to the top of Carr Peak veers right. The demanding route climbs a third of a mile. Along the way, watch for **Lemmon's sage, hawk weed,** and **Mexican silene**. Just below the cobble-covered peak, watch for **Geyer's onion, large-flowered brickellbush,** and **many-flowered gromwell**.

Once on the peak, enjoy the view of Sierra Vista and the surrounding mountains, then return the way you came.

Blankets of wildflowers spread over ponderosa park meadows
along the Rainbow Rim Trail in northern Arizona.

APPENDIX A: *Common/Scientific Wildfower Names*

adder's mouth (*Malaxis soulei*)

ageratina (*Ageratina herbacea*)

agrimonia (*Agrimonia striata*)

alfalfa (*Medicago sativa*)

alpine goldenrod (*Solidago sp.*)

alumroot (*Heuchera versicolor*)

American basketflower (*Centaurea americana*)

amber lily (*Anthericum torreyi*)

antelope horns (*Asclepias asperula*)

antelope sage (*Eriogonum jamesii*)

Apache plume (*Fallugia paradoxa*)

Arizona bladderpod (*Lesquerella arizonica*)

Arizona cudweed (*Gnaphalium arizonicum*)

Arizona peavine (*Lathyrus arizonicus*)

Arizona rose (*Rosa arizonica*)

Arizona thistle (*Cirsium arizonicum*)

aspen fleabane (*Erigeron macranthus*)

banana yucca (*Yucca baccata*)

baneberry (*Actaea rubra*)

bergamot (*Monarda menthaefolia*)

bigleaf avens (*Geum macrophyllum*)

birdsfoot lotus (*Lotus corniculatus*)

birdsfoot morning glory (*Ipomoea leptotoma*)

blackbrush (*Coleogyne ramosissima*)

blackfoot daisy (*Melampodium leucanthum*)

black medick (*Medicago lupulina*)

blue Dicks (*Dichelostemma pulchellum/ rodiaea pulchella*)

blue elderberry (*Sambucus glauca*)

bouvardia (*Bouvardia glaberrima*)

bracken fern (*Pteridium aquilinum*)

bracted strawberry (*Fragaria bracteata*)

bristly hiddenflower (*Cryptantha setosissima*)

brown-eyed Susan (*Rudbeckia laciniata*)

bushy linarioides (*Penstemon linarioides*)

butter and eggs (*Linaria dalmatica*)

buttercup (*Ranunculus sp.*)

butterfly weed (*Asclepias tuberosa*)

Canada violet (*Viola canadensis*)

canaigre (*Rumex hymenosepalus*)

cane cholla (*Opuntia spinosior*)

canyon grape (*Vitis arizonica*)

cardinal flower (*Lobelia cardinalis*)

chicory (*Cichorium intybus*)

cinquefoil (*Potentilla sp.*)

clammyweed (*Polanisia trachysperma*)

claret cup cactus (*Echinocereus sp.*)

claret cups (*Echinocereus triglochidiatus* var. *melanacanthus*)

cleavers (*Galium aparine*)

cliff fendler bush (*Fendlera rupicola*)

cliff rock cress (*Arabis perennans*)

cliff rose (*Cowania mexicana* var. *stansburiana*)

clustered broom rape (*Orobanche fasciculata* var. *lutea*)

Cockerell's sedum (*Sedum cockerellii*)

common mallow (*Malva neglecta*)

common monkey flower (*Mimulus guttatus*)

common snakeweed (*Gutierrezia sarothrae*)

Cooper's goldflower (*Hymenoxys cooperi*)

coral bells (*Heuchera sanguinea*)

cosmos (*Cosmos parviflorus*)

Coulter's lupine (*Lupinus sparsiflorus*)

cow clover (*Trifolium pinetorum*)

cow parsnip (*Heracleum lanatum*)

creeping barberry (*Berberis repens*)

crimson monkey flower (*Mimulus cardinalis*)

curlycup gumweed (*Grindelia squarrosa*)

curly dock (*Rumex crispus*)

currant (*Ribes sp.*)

daylily (*Lilium sp.*)

death camas (*Zigadenus virescens*)

deerbrush (*Ceanothus integerrimus*)

desert blazing star (*Mentzelia pumila*)

desert marigold (*Baileya multiradiata*)

desert senna (*Cassia covesii*)

devil's claw (*Proboscidea parviflora*)

dodder (*Cuscuta indecora*)

dogbane (*Apocynum sp.*)

Douglas' water hemlock (*Cicuta douglasii*)

dwarf goldenrod (*Solidago decumbens*)

dwarf rattlesnake plantain (*Goodyera repens*)

egg mat buckwheat (*Eriogonum ovalifolium*)

elegant camus (*Zigadenus elegans*)

elkslip (*Caltha leptosepala*)

Emory's comet milkweed (*Asclepias sp.*)

Engelmann's prickly pear (*Opuntia phaeacantha*)

ephedra (*Ephedra trifurca*)

eryngo (*Eryngium heterophyllum*)

evening primrose (*Oenothera sp.*)

false hellebore (*Veratrum californicum*)

false Solomon's seal (*Smilacina racemosa*)

false toadflax (*Comandra pallida*)

feather dalea (*Dalea sp.*)

Fendler rose (*Rosa fendleri*)

Fendler's ceanothus (*Ceanothus fendleri*)

Fendler's hawkweed (*Hieracium fendleri*)

Fendler's potato (*Solanum fendleri*)

Fendler's sandwort (*Arenaria fendleri*)

fernbush (*Chamaebatiaria millefolium*)

field mint (*Mentha arvensis*)

fine-leaf woollywhite (*Hymenopappus filifolius*)

fireweed (*Epilobium angustifolium*)

flannel bush (*Fremontia californica*)

fleabane (*Erigeron sp.*)

foothill kittentails (*Besseya plantaginea*)

four-winged saltbrush (*Atriplex canescens*)

Franciscan bluebell (*Mertensia franciscana*)

gentiana (*Gentiana heterosepala*)

Geyer's onion (*Allium geyeri*)

giant hyssop (*Agastache urticifolia*)

giant rattlesnake plantain (*Goodyera oblongifolia*)

golden aster (*Heterotheca sp.*)

golden-beard penstemon (*Penstemon barbatus*)

golden draba (*Draba aurea*)

goldeneye (*Viguiera sp.*)

golden-flowered agave (*Agave palmeri* var. *chrysantha*)

goldenrod (*Solidago sp.*)

goldenweed (*Haplopappus gracilis*)

goldflower (*Hymenoxys sp.*)

goosefoot (*Chenopodium album*)

Graham's tick clover (*Desmodium grahami*)

grand collomia (*Collomia grandiflora*)

Gray's lima bean (*Phaseolus grayanus*)

Gray's lousewort (*Pedicularis grayi*)

green-flowered macromeria (*Macromeria viridiflora*)

green gentian (*Frasera speciosa*)

green leaf manzanita (*Arctostaphylos patula*)

green pyrola (*Pyrola chlorantha*)

groundsel (*Senecio sp.*)

gum weed (*Grindelia squarrosa*)

harebell (*Campanula rotundifolia*)

heal all (*Prunella vulgaris*)

Hill's lupine (*Lupinus hillii*)

Himalaya berry (*Rubus procerus*)

hooded ladies' tresses (*Spiranthes romanzoffiana*)

Hooker's evening primrose (*Oenothera hookeri*)

hop vine (*Humulus americanus*)

horehound (*Marrubium vulgare*)

horsetail (*Equisetum arvense*)

Indian paintbrush (*Castilleja sp.*)

lady fern (*Athyrium felix-femina*)

Lambert's locoweed (*Oxytropis lambertii*)

large-flowered brickellbush (*Brickellia grandiflora*)

larkspur (*Delphinium sp.*)

Lemmon's sage (*Salvia lemmonii*)

lilac chaste tree (*Vitex agnus-castus*)

little leaf globemallow (*Sphaeralcea parvifolia*)

locoweed (*Astragalus sp.*)

many-flowered gilia (*Gilia multiflora*)

many-flowered gromwell (*Lithospermum multiflorum*)

many-flowered stick seed (*Hackelia sp.*)

meadow rue (*Thalictrum fendleri*)

Mexican elderberry (*Sambucus mexicana*)

Mexican hat (*Ratibida columnaris* var. *pulcherrima*)

Mexican silene (*Silene laciniata*)

Mexican woollywhite (*Hymenopappus mexicanus*)

milkwort (*Polygala alba*)

miner's lettuce (*Claytonia perfoliata*)

mistletoe (*Phoradendron sp.*)

Mogollon Indian paintbrush (*Castilleja mogollonica*)

monkshood (*Aconitum columbianum*)

mountain ash (*Sorbus dumosa*)

mountain lobelia (*Lobelia anatina*)

mountain lover (*Pachystima myrsinites*)

mountain mahogany (*Cercocarpus sp.*)

mountain ninebark (*Physocarpus monogynus*)

mountain parsley (*Pseudocymopterus montanus*)

mountain spray (*Holodiscus dumosus*)

mountain thistle (*Cirsium sp.*)

mouse-ear chickweed (*Cerastium vulgatum*)

mullein (*Verbascum thapsus*)

narrow-leaf penstemon *(Penstemon linarioides)*
narrow-leaf tick clover *(Cologania longifolia)*
New Mexico checkermallow *(Sidalcea neomexicana)*
New Mexico groundsel *(Senecio neomexicanus)*
New Mexico locust *(Robinia neomexicana)*
New Mexico raspberry *(Rubus neomexicanus)*
New Mexico vervain *(Verbena macdougalii)*
New Mexico yellow flax *(Linum neomexicanum)*
nightshade *(Solanum sp.)*
nodding groundsel *(Senecio bigelovii)*
nodding onion *(Allium cernuum)*
Nuttall's linanthus *(Linanthastrum nuttallii)*
orange agoseris *(Agoseris aurantiaca)*
orange gooseberry *(Ribes pinetorum)*
osha *(Ligusticum porteri)*
Palmer's penstemon *(Penstemon palmeri)*
paperflower *(Psilostrophe tagetina)*
Parry pedicularis *(Pedicularis parryi)*
Parry's agave *(Agave parryi)*
Parry's bellflower *(Campanula parryi)*
Parry's primrose *(Primula parryi)*
pearly everlasting *(Anaphalis margaritacea)*
phlox *(Phlox sp.)*
pinesap *(Monotropa latisquama)*
pine trumpet *(Polemonium pauciflorum)*
pink windmill *(Sisymbrium linearifolium)*
plains beebalm *(Monarda pectinata)*
pleated gentian *(Gentiana affinis)*
point leaf manzanita *(Arctostaphylos sp.)*
poison ivy *(Rhus radicans)*
poison milkweed *(Asclepias subverticillata)*
polemonium *(Polemonium sp.)*
porch penstemon *(Penstemon strictus)*
prairie smoke *(Geum triflorum)*
prairie sunflower *(Helianthus petiolaris)*
princely daisy *(Erigeron formosissimus)*
prostrate vervain *(Verbena bracteata)*
purple gilia *(Ipomopsis thurberi)*
purple vetch *(Vicia americana)*
purslane *(Portulaca suffrutescens)*
pussytoes *(Antennaria rosulata)*
quinine bush *(Garrya flavescens)*
rattlesnake weed *(Euphorbia albomarginata)*
red cinquefoil *(Potentilla thurberi)*
red-dome blanketflower *(Gaillardia pinnatifida)*

red elderberry *(Sambucus racemosa)*
red figwort *(Scrophularia coccinea)*
red-osier dogwood *(Cornus stolonifera)*
red raspberry *(Rubus idaeus)*
red-root buckwheat *(Eriogonum racemosum)*
Richardson's geranium *(Geranium richardsonii)*
rock echeveria *(Dudleya saxosa)*
rockmat *(Petrophytum caespitosum)*
Rocky Mountain beebalm *(Cleome serrulata)*
Rocky Mountain columbine *(Aquilegia pinetorum)*
Rocky Mountain iris *(Iris missouriensis)*
sacred datura *(Datura meteloides)*
sagebrush *(Artemisia sp.)*
St. John's wort *(Hypericum formosum)*
sandpuff *(Tripterocalyx carnea)*
sandwort *(Arenaria sp.)*
saxifrage *(Saxifraga sp.)*
scarlet creeper *(Ipomoea coccinea)*
scarlet gaura *(Gaura coccinea)*
scarlet monkey flower *(Mimulus cardinalis)*
Scouler's catchfly *(Silene scouleri)*
scruffy prairie clover *(Dalea albiflora)*
sego lily *(Calochortus nuttallii)*
shooting star *(Dodecatheon sp.)*
showy milkweed *(Asclepias speciosa)*
shrubby cinquefoil *(Potentilla fruticosa)*
sida *(Sida procumbens)*
side-bell pyrola *(Ramischia secunda)*
silverleaf nightshade *(Solanum elaeagnifolium)*
silver-stem lupine *(Lupinus argenteus)*
skunkbush *(Rhus trilobata)*
skyrocket *(Ipomopsis aggregata)*
slender bog orchid *(Habenaria sp.)*
smartweed *(Polygonum sp.)*
snapdragon vine *(Maurandya antirrhiniflora)*
sneezeweed *(Helenium hoopesii)*
snowberry *(Symphoricarpos sp.)*
sotol *(Dasylirion wheeleri)*
spiny cliffbrake fern *(Pellaea longimucronata)*
spotted water hemlock *(Cicuta maculata)*
spreading four o'clock *(Mirabilis oxybaphoides)*
spur gentian *(Halenia recurva)*
squaw currant *(Ribes inebrians)*
squawroot *(Conopholis mexicana)*
star cloak fern *(Notholaena standleyi)*

star gilia *(Gilia sp.)*

star Solomon's seal *(Smilacina stellata)*

stemless evening primrose *(Oenothera caespitosa)*

sugar sumac *(Rhus ovata)*

sunbright *(Talinum parviflorum)*

sunflower *(Helianthus annuus)*

sweet Cicely *(Osmorhiza depauperata)*

sweet clover vetch *(Vicia pulchella)*

sweet scent *(Hedeoma hyssopifolium)*

tansyleaf spine aster *(Aster tanacetifolius)*

tansy mustard *(Descurainia richardsonii)*

taperleaf *(Pericome caudata)*

Texas betony *(Stachys coccinea)*

thermopsis *(Thermopsis pinetorum)*

thimbleberry *(Rubus parviflorus var. parvifolius)*

thistle *(Cirsium sp.)*

Thurber's gilia *(Ipomopsis thurberi)*

Thurber's stephanomeria
    (Stephanomeria thurberi)

tower daisy *(Townsendia formosa)*

towering polemonium *(Polemonium foliosissimum)*

Townsendia daisy *(Townsendia excapa)*

trailing four o'clock *(Allionia incarnata)*

twinberry *(Lonicera involucrata)*

two-tone owl's clover *(Orthocarpus purpureo-albus)*

Utah serviceberry *(Amelanchier utahensis)*

Utah swertia *(Swertia utahensis)*

verbena *(Verbena sp.)*

verileaf phacelia *(Phacelia heterophylla)*

Virginia creeper *(Parthenocissus inserta)*

virgin's bower *(Clematis ligusticifolia)*

wandbloom penstemon *(Penstemon virgatus)*

watercress *(Nasturtium officinale)*

waterleaf *(Hydrophyllum sp.)*

western bistort *(Polygonum bistortoides)*

western blue flax *(Linum lewisii)*

western dayflower *(Commelina sp.)*

western peppergrass *(Lepidium sp.)*

western redbud *(Cercis occidentalis)*

western wallflower *(Erysimum capitatum)*

Wheeler thistle *(Cirsium sp.)*

Whipple's penstemon *(Penstemon whippleanus)*

white ball acacia *(Acacia angustissima)*

white evening primrose *(Oenothera sp.)*

white milkwort *(Polygala alba)*

white nightshade *(Solanum nodiflorum)*

white prairie clover *(Petalostemum occidentale)*

white shooting star *(Dodecatheon dentatum)*

white snakeroot *(Eupatorium sp.)*

white top clover *(Trifolium repens)*

whorled milkweed *(Asclepias verticillata)*

wild buckwheat *(Eriogonum sp.)*

wild celery *(Apium graveolens)*

wild chrysanthemum *(Bahia dissecta)*

wild four o'clock *(Mirabilis multiflora)*

wild geranium *(Geranium caespitosum)*

wild parsley *(Lomatium sp.)*

wild strawberry *(Fragaria ovalis)*

willow weed *(Epilobium halleanum)*

winged buckwheat *(Eriogonum alatum)*

Woodhouse's phlox *(Phlox woodhousei)*

woodland pinedrops *(Pterospora andromedea)*

wood sorrel *(Oxalis decaphylla)*

woolly morning glory *(Ipomoea dessertorum)*

Wright beeflower *(Hymenothrix wrightii)*

Wright's bluets *(Houstonia wrightii)*

Wright's deervetch *(Lotus wrightii)*

yarrow *(Achillea millefolium var. lanulosa)*

yellow columbine *(Aquilegia chrysantha)*

yellow evening primrose *(Oenothera sp.)*

yellow-eyed grass *(Sisyrinchium arizonicum)*

yellow-flowered buckwheat *(Eriogonum sp.)*

yellow menodora *(Menodora scabra)*

yellow pond lily *(Nuphar polysepalum)*

yerba santa *(Eriodictyon angustifolium)*

APPENDIX B: *Hikes by Difficulty*

The hikes in this book are all day hikes, and many trails are rated as easy or moderate. You can skim this list to find trails in your area that are suited to your hiking ability. Please note these are subjective ratings —one person's leisurely hike may be another's marathon trek. Check elevation ranges, trail lengths, and the descriptions for particular hikes to help you gauge the effort required. If you're a novice hiker, you may want to start out with itineraries described as having well-marked trails with little grade. But if you're an experienced hiker seeking adventure, look to the difficult hikes that feature rock-hopping and steep canyon descents. You may like to try a few to assess your own level; most of all, enjoy the experience!

Easy Hikes

NORTHERN ARIZONA
3. Big Ridge Tank: Arizona Trail
5. North Rainbow Trail (by boat shuttle)
10. Sandy's Canyon Trail
14. Red Mountain Trail
15. Slate Mountain Trail
16. Upper West Fork of Oak Creek

CENTRAL ARIZONA
17. West Fork Trail
18. Wilson Canyon Trail
23. Canyon Creek
25. Parker Creek Canyon Overlook

EASTERN ARIZONA
33. Thompson Trail
34. West Baldy Trail (first 1.7 miles)
35. East Baldy Trail (first 0.75 mile)
36. Butler Canyon Nature Trail

SOUTHEASTERN ARIZONA
38. Upper Grant Creek
40. Vault Mine Trail
41. Marshall Gulch Trail
42. Upper Sabino Canyon Riparian Area
44. Meadow Trail
45. Oracle Ridge Trail
46. Road to Mount Bigelow

Moderate Hikes

NORTHERN ARIZONA
1. Parissawampitts Point: Rainbow Rim Trail
2. Crystal Spring: Arizona Trail
4. Widforss Trail
6. Sycamore Rim Trail
7. Kendrick Mountain Trail
8. Inner Basin Trail
11. Walnut Canyon Overlook: Arizona Trail
12. Fisher Point: Arizona Trail
15. Slate Mountain Trail

CENTRAL ARIZONA
20. See Canyon Trail
21. Horton Creek Trail
24. Sand Tank Canyon

EASTERN ARIZONA
26. Bear Wallow Trail
27. KP Creek Trail
28. Upper Fish Creek Trail
29. Lower Fish Creek Trail
30. South Fork Trail
31. Steeple Trail

SOUTHEASTERN ARIZONA
39. Crest Trail
47. Comfort Spring Trail

Strenuous Hikes

NORTHERN ARIZONA
5. North Rainbow Trail
   (hiking from trailhead to Rainbow Bridge)
9. Abineau Trail
13. Bismarck Lake Trail

CENTRAL ARIZONA
19. Barnhardt Trail
22. Pine Canyon Trail

EASTERN ARIZONA
32. Upper Grant Creek Trail
34. West Baldy Trail (miles 1.7–7)
35. East Baldy Trail (miles 0.75–7)

SOUTHEASTERN ARIZONA
37. Ash Creek Trail
43. Butterfly Trail
48. Carr Peak Trail

APPENDIX C: *Bibliography*

Angier, Bradford. *Field Guide to Medicinal Wild Plants*. Harrisburg, Pa.: Stackpole Books, 1978.

Arnberger, Leslie. *Flowers of the Southwest Mountains*. Tucson: Southwest Parks and Monuments Association, 1982.

Bernheimer, Charles L. *Rainbow Bridge*. Albuquerque: Center for Anthropological Studies, 1999.

Bowers, Janice Emily. *100 Desert Wildflowers of the Southwest*. Tucson: Southwest Parks and Monuments Association, 1989.

———. *100 Roadside Wildflowers of Southwest Woodlands*. Tucson: Southwest Parks and Monuments Association, 1987.

Brown, Tom, Jr. *Tom Brown's Guide to Wild Edible and Medicinal Plants*. New York: Berkley Books, 1985.

Duke, James A., Ph.D. *The Green Pharmacy*. Emmaus, Pa.: Rodale Press Inc., 1997.

Dykeman, Peter A., and Thomas S. Elias. *Field Guide to North American Edible Wild Plants*. New York: Outdoor Life Books, 1982.

Epple, Anne Orth, and Lewis E. Epple. *A Field Guide to the Plants of Arizona*. Helena, Mont.: Falcon Press Publishing Company, Inc., 1997.

Fagan, Damian. *Canyon Country Wildflowers*. Helena, Mont.: Falcon Press Publishing Company, Inc., 1998.

Granger, Byrd Howell. *Arizona Names: X Marks the Place*. Tucson: The Falconer Publishing Company, 1983.

Leavengood, Betty. *Tucson Hiking Guide*. Boulder, Colo.: Pruett Publishing Company, 1991.

Lincoff, Gary H. *National Audubon Society Field Guide to North American Mushrooms*. New York: Alfred A. Knopf, Inc., 1981.

Lust, John. *The Herb Book*. Simi Valley, Calif.: Benedict Lust Publications, 1974.

Mayes, Vernon O., and Barbara Bayless Lacy. *Nanise'—A Navajo Herbal*. Tsaile, Ariz.: Navajo Community College Press, 1989.

Molvar, Erik. *Hiking Arizona's Cactus Country*. Helena, Mont.: Falcon Press Publishing Company, Inc., 1995.

Niehaus, Theodore F., Charles L. Ripper, and Virginia Savage. *Southwestern and Texas Wildflowers*. New York: Houghton Mifflin Company, 1984.

Niering, William A., and Nancy C. Olmstead. *The Audubon Society Field Guide to North American Wildflowers: Eastern Region*. New York: Alfred A. Knopf, Inc., 1979.

Orlean, Susan. *The Orchid Thief*. New York: The Ballantine Publishing Group, 1998.

Spellenberg, Richard. *The Audubon Society Field Guide to North American Wildflowers: Western Region*. New York: Alfred A. Knopf, Inc., 1979.

Taylor, Leonard. *The Hiker's Guide to the Huachuca Mountains*. Sierra Vista, Ariz.: Thunder Peak Productions, 1991.

Tweit, Susan J. *The Great Southwest Nature Fact Book*. Seattle: Alaska Northwest Books, 1992.

———. *Meet the Wild Southwest*. Seattle: Alaska Northwest Books, 1995.

Wells, Diana. *100 Flowers and How They Got Their Names*. Chapel Hill, N.C.: Algonquin Books of Chapel Hill, 1997.

Index

photo by Catherine Ryan/Novica.com

ABOUT THE AUTHOR
Christine Maxa

Christine is the author of *Arizona's Best Wildflower Hikes, The Desert* and *Arizona's Best Autumn Color: 50 Great Hikes*. An award-winning freelance writer, she has written for *Arizona Highways, Backpacker Magazine, National Geographic Traveler,* and *Southwest Art* among other national and regional publications, and she has been featured on radio and TV. She wrote the "Hike of the Week" column for the daily *Arizona Republic* for more than two years and is the executive assistant on the Advisory Committee for the Arizona State Committee on Trails. She currently writes a hiking column for *Arizona Living* magazine.